T0338818

PRIME
MINISTERS

PRIME MINISTERS

JONATHAN BASTABLE

RYDON
PUBLISHING

A Rydon Publishing Book
35 The Quadrant
Hassocks
West Sussex
BN6 8BP

www.rydonpublishing.co.uk
www.rydonpublishing.com

Revised edition first published by Rydon Publishing in 2019
First published by David & Charles in 2011

A CIP catalogue record for this book is available from the British Library.

ISBN: 978-1-910821-220

Printed in Poland by BZGraf S.A.

CONTENTS

INTRODUCTION

Perhaps the strangest of the many strange facts about the British prime minister is that the job does not really exist. Constitutionally, there is no such thing as a PM. The man (or woman) in Number Ten Downing Street is First Lord of the Treasury – no more, no less – and the role of prime minister is not so much an office of state as a convention, a long-standing custom – a bit like the Christmas tree in Trafalgar Square.

The role of prime minister as we now understand it evolved slowly and organically over two centuries. At first, the prime minister was merely the chief among several ministers, the first to be summoned into the presence of the king or queen when the sovereign had something to say. This was certainly the way it worked with Robert Walpole, the man generally held to be the first PM. Interestingly, when Walpole met with George I, the two men spoke to each other in Latin, since German-born George knew little English. It was a tortuous way to conduct business, and it inclined George to leave the running of the country to Walpole, who clearly knew what he was doing. This abrogation of authority was one of many small circumstances that, over the decades, shifted the locus of political power in Britain from the royal throne to a lonely desk in an upstairs room on Downing Street.

Some 18th-century prime ministers refused to be known by the term prime minister, because they sensed that there was something pejorative about it, a hint of power-hungriness that was unbecoming to a gentleman. This odd coyness about the title has made the job of prime minister difficult to define, even in modern times, and many PMs and observers have had to resort to all manner of metaphors in order to make sense of it. John Morley, a minister in the government of Henry Campbell-Bannerman, said that 'the prime minister is the keystone of the cabinet arch' – a straighforward architectural analogy that anyone can understand.

Winston Churchill said rather more obscurely that 'we propose to give the people a lighthouse, not a shop window,' – meaning that a prime minister's job is primarily to provide the people with guidance from afar, and that the general public (that is to say, the voters who put the prime minister in office) probably shouldn't be allowed to inspect the processes and the products of government too closely.

Harold Wilson, who thought more deeply about the nature of the premiership than any modern prime minister, had this to say about his impending election: 'Whereas in the 1960s I had played in every position on the field – goalkeeper, midfield, taking penalties and corners and bringing on the lemons – I was going to be an old-fashioned centre-half, lying well back, feeding the ball to those whose job it was to score goals, and moving upfield only for rare set-piece occasions.' He meant oranges, by the way: PMs don't get much time for Sunday football. As for the rest of that over-extended analogy, what he meant is anybody's guess.

So what are prime ministers for, and what makes the position so extraordinary? The best summation was given by Benjamin Disraeli. He captured the paradoxes and peculiarity of the job when he said: 'I follow the people – for am I not their leader?'

Man of the Forest
Disraeli's passion for trees

Benjamin Disraeli was a lifelong dendrophile: there was nothing he loved more than a fine tree. Whereas his great rival WE Gladstone delighted in chopping them down, Disraeli loved to plant them. Some of Disraeli's best mature writing was dendrological. 'A forest is monotonous only to the ignorant,' he wrote, 'It is a life of ceaseless variety,' – rather like politics, he might have added. This is Disraeli's evocative description of the trees at Hughenden, his Buckinghamshire estate, as he saw them in October 1858. 'We were absent nearly a fortnight, and I find a great difference in the colour of the trees – the limes all golden, the beeches ruddy brown, while the oaks and elms and pines are still dark

Benjamin Disraeli

and green, and contrast well with the brighter tints. But not a leaf has fallen; they want the first whisper of the frost and then they will go out like lamps when the dawn breaks on a long festival...'

Trees seemed to have the power to restore Disraeli's weary soul. At the end of the long and exhausting parliamentary session he would always retire to Hughenden specifically to commune with his sylvan friends. 'When I come down to Hughenden I pass the first week in sauntering about my park and examining all my trees, and then I saunter in the library and survey the books.' During that first week he would spend some of the time talking to woodsmen ('Their conversation is most interesting; Nature whispers to them many of her secrets.') Disraeli often marked the visit of an important person by planting a tree in their honour. He specifically stated in his will that no trees on the estate were ever to be cut down, but he had planted so many sapling tributes to distinguished overnighters that, after his death, the grounds of Hughenden began to look like an overgrown primeval forest. So in the event, many of the trees that Disraeli had put in were felled (Gladstone-style) after all.

HELLO, TREES

Henry Campbell-Bannerman was another prime minister with an inordinate fondness for trees. He was in the habit of bowing and wishing good morning to any specimen that struck him as particularly fine.

Henry Campbell-Bannerman

Idle Jim
James Callaghan's first days in the job

Y ou would think that a prime minister's first days in Number Ten Downing Street would be spent frantically learning the ropes, that the new PM would have to devote a good deal of time and effort to getting to grips with the levers of power. But this is not always so: one of the first discoveries that freshly elected prime ministers make is that their new job is one of the loneliest in the world.

'I had nothing to do,' recalled James Callaghan (he was elevated from foreign secretary to prime minister in April 1976, when Harold Wilson suddenly resigned the post). 'Ministers were busy with their departmental work. The phone did not ring for, generally speaking, people do not telephone the prime minister – the prime minister telephones them. For a brief period I savoured the suspicion that as everyone else was doing the government's work, I could be the idlest member of the administration if I was so minded. '

Speak As You Think…
and Cherish Freedom
The mottoes of prime ministers

Prime ministers are entitled to a motto if they are born peers (as many have been) or if they are awarded a peerage in recognition of their service to the nation. A motto may also be adopted by a Knight of the Garter – which is how Edward Heath, for example, came by his. Some former prime ministers do not qualify, because they continued to be commoners after leaving office. Among them are Andrew Bonar Law, Ramsay MacDonald and Tony Blair.

LORD SALISBURY
Sero sed serio
Late, but in earnest

MARGARET THATCHER
Cherish Freedom

JAMES CALLAGHAN
Malo laborare quam languere
Better to work than to be idle

ALEC DOUGLAS-HOME
True to the end

CLEMENT ATTLEE
Sursum corda
Lift up your hearts

LORD RUSSELL
Che sara sara
What will be will be

WINSTON CHURCHILL
Fiel pero desdichado
Faithful though unfortunate

EARL OF WILMINGTON
Je ne cherche que un
I seek but one

LORD PALMERSTON
Flecti non frangi
To bend, but not to break

HAROLD WILSON
Tempus rerum imperator
Time is the ruler of all things

DUKE OF NEWCASTLE
Vincit amor patriae
Love of country conquers all

DUKE OF PORTLAND
Craignez honte
Fear shame

ROBERT WALPOLE
Fari quae sentiat
Speak as you think

NEVILLE CHAMBERLAIN
Je tiens ferme
I stand fast

WILLIAM PITT THE YOUNGER
Benigno numine
By benign providence

ARTHUR BALFOUR
Virtus ad aethera tendit
Virtue reaches to heaven

LORD NORTH
La vertu est la seule noblesse
Virtue is the only nobility

DAVID LLOYD GEORGE
Y gwir yn erbyn y byd
The truth against the world

EARL OF DERBY
Sans changer
Without changing

SPENCER PERCEVAL
Sub cruce candida
Under the white cross

STANLEY BALDWIN
Per deum meum transilio murum
With God's help, I shall jump the wall

BENJAMIN DISRAELI
Forti nihil difficile
All is easy to the brave

EARL GREY
De bon vouloir servir le roy
To serve the king with a good will

HENRY CAMPBELL-BANNERMAN
Ne obliviscaris
Do not forget

GEORGE GRENVILLE
Pro deo, patria et amicis
For my God, for my country, and for my friends

EDWARD HEATH
Plus fait douceur que violence
Gentleness achieves more than violence

DUKE OF WELLINGTON
Virtutis fortuna comes
Fortune favours the brave

Long Odds at Number Ten

The huge unlikelihood of anyone ever becoming prime minister

It is surely true that most MPs enter parliament harbouring a vague hope that perhaps, one day, they will become prime minister. But the harsh statistical fact of the matter is that they almost certainly won't. The statistical truth is that 99.7 per cent of members of parliament never make it to the very top of the governmental tree. To become PM you have to be extremely ambitious or else amazingly lucky – or maybe both.

Let's take a look at the odds in historical terms.

Tony Blair (above) and his successor Gordon Brown (left)

Clement Attlee

Among the 640 MPs elected to the first post-war parliament in 1945 there were four future prime ministers: Anthony Eden, Harold Wilson, James Callaghan, and Winston Churchill – who had already held the post once. When Harold Wilson became PM in 1964 there were three future PMs in the house: Callaghan again – plus, on the opposition benches, Edward Heath and Margaret Thatcher. When Thatcher got the job in 1979 there was only one future incumbent elsewhere in the house, her immediate successor John Major. Two future PMs won seats in 1983: Tony Blair and Gordon Brown. Not a single prime minister has emerged from the parliamentary intake of 1987 or 1992.

Theresa May is so far, the only prime minister to have arisen from the draft of 1997. David Cameron and Boris Johnson both won seats in 2001.

It remains to be seen how many future prime ministers will have parliamentary careers dating back to 2005 or subsequent elections, but the chances are: not many.

Fleet Street

THE MANY LAYERS OF WINSTON

Clement Attlee, the future Labour prime minister, was Winston Churchill's deputy in the wartime coalition government. He had this to say about dealing with the complex personality of a great prime minister: 'There was a layer of seventeenth century, a layer of eighteenth century, a layer of nineteenth century, and possibly even a layer of twentieth century. You were never sure which layer would be uppermost.'

The Inventor of Spin
David Lloyd George and uses of the press

People tend to think that media spin and negative briefings are techniques that have only recently become available to prime ministers. But David Lloyd George was a master of the dark arts of news management, and used them mercilessly to do down or eliminate his enemies.

In the early years of World War I, when he was Secretary of State for

War, Lloyd George decided that he would like to sack General Haig, who was then commander-in-chief of British forces in France. Haig was well liked by the public, and it would have caused an outcry if he had been dismissed out of hand. So Lloyd George approached Lord Northcliffe, proprietor of *The Times, The Daily Mail* and several other newspapers. 'The little man came to see me,' recounted Lord Northcliffe, with evident distaste, 'And told me that he would like to get rid of Haig, but that he could not do so as he was too popular. He made the proposition that I should attack him in my group of newspapers and so render him unpopular enough to be dealt with. "You kill him and I will bury him." Those were his very words.'

'I Am Murdered, Murdered…'
The strange assassination of Spencer Perceval

There have been many attempts on the lives of prime minister down the decades. In 1984, the Provisional IRA planted a bomb

at the Grand Hotel in Brighton; they were aiming to kill Margaret Thatcher, who was staying there for the duration of the Conservative party conference. In 1991, the Provisionals made an attempt on the life of John Major. They fired three mortar shells at Downing Street from the back of a van parked in Whitehall; one bomb landed in the back garden of Number Ten and rattled the windows of the Cabinet room, where Major was in session with his ministers.

So prime ministers have always been potential targets for assassins, but only one prime minister has ever

Spencer Perceval

been killed by an attacker. He was Spencer Perceval, and the strange and tragic manner of his death is now practically the only thing that he is remembered for.

Spencer Perceval was perhaps the most gentle and godly prime minister ever to serve his country, and this somehow makes his violent demise all the more shocking. On the day he was to die, Monday May 11, 1812, he spent the morning at home, preparing for an important debate. He got so bound up in his work that he forgot the time, and set off late for the House. His friend, the abolitionist William Wilberforce, spotted him hurrying along Downing Street, and was moved to 'an affectionate eulogy on his worth and principles'. When Perceval arrived at the Palace of Westminster he left his cloak and stick with an attendant and went upstairs towards the lobby. He passed a journalist named William Jerdan, who held open a door for him. The prime minister smiled his thanks.

As Perceval stepped into the crowded lobby he was approached by a man who produced a pistol from his clothing, pressed its barrel to Perceval's chest, and fired a shot. The assailant then calmly stepped away and sat down on a nearby bench. As for Perceval, he lurched forward and collapsed to the floor. An MP named William Smith was standing nearby. He turned round on hearing the shot, and to his horror the wounded prime minister fell at his feet. Smith heard Perceval gasp: 'Oh, I am murdered, murdered…' William Smith and another man lifted Perceval from the floor and carried him to a small room known as the Secretary's Office. There they laid him on a table. A trickle of blood was flowing from the prime minister's mouth. He groaned once or twice, then his head flopped to one side. He was dead.

His attacker, meanwhile, was still sitting quietly on a bench in the lobby. A crowd gathered round him, and one of those present recognised him as John Bellingham, a businessman. Bellingham had been petitioning parliament for months because he felt he was due compensation for money he had lost through a failed commercial venture in Russia. A day or two before the shooting, he had been seen in the public gallery of the Commons, where he had spent his time peering at the prime minister through a pair of opera glasses. William Jerdan, the journalist who was suddenly the last friendly person to have seen Perceval alive, now took it upon himself to go through Bellingham's pockets. He found those opera glasses, along with the murder weapon, a second loaded pistol, and a considerable quantity of small change. Disarmed and unresisting, John Bellingham was taken away and locked up by the serjeant-at-arms.

By this time, news of the murder had spread beyond the Palace of Westminster. The poet Samuel Taylor Coleridge heard of it on the street, and was shocked to see that the lower orders were jubilant, as if a tyrant had been overthrown. Bonfires were lit and drums were beaten in the Midlands and the North. This unexpected reaction made some fear that the shooting was the signal for a revolution, and a few timid aristocratic types made plans to flee the country. But no revolutionary spark took hold; in fact, everything that followed was a sad anti-climax.

Spencer Perceval, having died on Monday, was buried the following Saturday. The funeral was a private ceremony, with little pomp. As for Bellingham, he was tried at the Old Bailey on the day before the funeral, and found guilty in the course of the morning. He was executed on the Monday, exactly a week after committing his crime and making his little mark on history. His clothes were auctioned off; it was said that someone paid ten pounds for the privilege of owning his greatcoat.

Winston Churchill

Churchillian, but not Churchill
Five things Churchill is said to have said, but didn't

Churchill is the most quotable of prime ministers – so much so that there are lots of forgeries about. Some of these fake *dicta* are pretty convincing. Here are five of the best:

'The only traditions of the Royal Navy are rum, sodomy and the lash.' Churchill never said this, but once remarked that he wished he had.

★

'If you're not a liberal when you're 25, you have no heart. If you're not a conservative by the time you're 35, you have no brain'. It has been pointed out that Churchill himself was a Liberal when he was 35.

★

'The hardest cross I have to bear is the Cross of Lorraine.' This is a wrongly attributed dig at General de Gaulle. The person who actually said it was General Edward Spears, Churchill's liaison officer with the Free French.

★

'All this contains much that is obviously true, and much that is relevant; unfortunately, what is obviously true is not relevant, and what is relevant is not obviously true.' This is only half-Churchill at most, since when he said it he was slightly misquoting one of his predecessors as PM, Arthur Balfour. What Balfour had said was: 'There were some things that were true, and some things that were trite; but what was true was trite, and what was not trite was not true'. Churchill's misremembered version is arguably better, and certainly more quotable.

★

'With integrity, nothing else counts. Without integrity, nothing else counts.' There is simply no record of Churchill ever saying any such thing.

Whips and Wicked Women
The peccadilloes of William Ewart Gladstone

Even by Victorian standards of piety, William Gladstone was an extremely religious man. He firmly believed that his political career was guided from on high, that a higher intelligence 'seems to sustain and spare me for some purpose of His own, deeply unworthy as I know myself to be.'

Gladstone's tendency to ascribe his successes and victories to divine influence infuriated his political opponents. 'I have no objection to Gladstone's habit of concealing the ace of trumps up his sleeve,' said one of his enemies, 'but I do object to his reiterated claim that it has been put there by Almighty God.' The novelist Emily Eden objected not so much to his religiosity as to his unremitting seriousness. 'If he were soaked in boiling water and rinsed until he were twisted into a rope, I do not suppose a drop of fun would ooze out,' she wrote. Benjamin Disraeli's verdict on Gladstone was just as cutting, but even more terse: 'He has not a single redeeming defect.'

Gladstone himself would not have agreed with Disraeli's judgment. One consequence of his darkly pious attitude to life was that he thought himself to be almost irredeemably sinful. He kept a detailed account of all his secret wrongdoings, chief

among which was a shameful fondness for mildly titillating French novels. He suffered paroxysms of guilt every time he indulged in salacious reading, and recorded the occasions in his meticulous diary as 'black days', and marked them with a cross. For a while he was in the habit of atoning for his sins by scourging himself (these occasions were indicated in the diary with a little drawing of a whip).

The self-flagellation might have been very damaging to Gladstone's political career had it ever come to light. It never did in Gladstone's lifetime – but he had another, much more public interest in sin, salvation and semi-detached sex –one that constantly threatened to impact on his personal and political reputation. This was his practice of wandering London's red light district with a view to rescuing prostitutes. He would go out into the streets around Piccadilly Circus, wait until he was propositioned, then accompany the lady back to her lodgings for long impassioned talks. He saw this as a kind of missionary work, and there is no question that he put many 'fallen women' in touch with charitable organisations that helped them achieve a better life. In many ways it was also a brave activity for Gladstone to take on: few other politicians, then or now, would have put themselves at risk of the kind of rumour and backhand sniggering that this lifelong habit provoked. On one occasion in 1852 (when he was Chancellor of the Exchequer), Gladstone was spotted in the company of a prostitute by a young man named Wilson, who attempted to blackmail him on the spot, saying he would denounce him to *The Morning Herald*. The minister, the prostitute and the blackmailer

went to Vine Street together, where Wilson – who had lost his nerve along the way – was placed under arrest. Gladstone felt obliged to press charges so as to deter future blackmailers; the unfortunate young chancer was convicted, and sentenced to a year's hard labour.

Gladstone's indignant claims of propriety notwithstanding, it is certainly true that he got a kind of erotic thrill from his work with prostitutes, and that this was part of the reason he undertook it. His night-time walks (which were also, he insisted, healthy exercise) allowed him to indulge the suppressed and outlawed sexual part of his nature in a way that his religious mind could tolerate. This is not mere Freudian supposition; Gladstone knew very well what his psyche was up to. He wrote that his rescues were surely 'carnal' because otherwise 'the withdrawal of them would not leave such a void.' He developed occasional crushes on particular women, seeking them out night after night like a lovelorn teenager. One woman, named Elizabeth Collins, he was moved to describe as 'half a most lovely statue, beautiful beyond measure.' This diary entry was made in Italian, the language he used whenever he had a sexually charged thought to record, and in the original it reads almost like the opening line of a love poem: '*La meta di una statua bellissima, bella oltre misura.*'

You Probably Could Make it Up
Five fictional prime ministers

The office of prime minister is ripe for comedy – and for an obvious reason. It is a job that always ends in failure – all PMs get kicked out in the end – and there is nothing funnier in life (or at least in art) than a mighty pratfall.

Jim Hacker in
Yes, Prime Minister
Hacker, played on television by Paul Eddington, is a fearful, uncertain, operator – a kind of party-political Hamlet. He was at first a mere minister, head of a nebulous and wide-ranging 'Department of Administrative Affairs'. In this role, he served under an unspecified

PM who is never named, or even identified as a man or a woman. (The series first appeared during Margaret Thatcher's premiership; she said it was her favourite programme). In 1986, Hacker became Prime Minister, but his main problem continued to be the obstructive and wily Whitehall mandarin Sir Humphrey, who saw all political activity as a danger to his own comfortable life at the peak of the Civil Service.

Adam Lang in *The Ghost Writer*
The prime minister in Robert Harris's novel is a kind of ultra-glamorous version of Tony Blair. In the film version he is played by Piers Brosnan, an erstwhile James Bond. The political resemblance to Blair lies in the fact that he has taken Britain into an unpopular war, is accused by his enemies of war crimes, and is held to have been too willing to do the bidding of his American allies. The action of the film takes place at a time when Lang has recently left office, and is writing his memoirs – precisely Blair's situation at the time of the film's release. But that is where the similarities end: Harris was

not seriously suggesting that Blair's wife was a CIA agent, that there were secret messages encoded in his upcoming memoirs, or that anyone who gets close to the truth about him is likely to meet with an unfortunate and usually fatal accident.

Alan B'Stard in
The New Statesman

Alan Beresford B'stard, played by Rik Mayall, was a grotesque caricature of a ultra-right-wing Tory: pinstriped, arrogant, snobbish, callous, power-hungry, wealthy, sadistic, utterly contemptuous of the lower classes ('In the good old days you were poor, you got ill, and you died,' he says). For most of his TV incarnation B'Stard is a mere back-bench MP. It is not until the last episode of the last series that he achieves PM status, and promptly has himself declared 'Lord Protector' in the manner of Oliver Cromwell. B'Stard's satirical value diminished somewhat when the Tories lost power in 1997. He was reinvented by the writers of the series as a kind of eminence grise behind New Labour, manipulating the new government from Number Nine Downing Street,

an address that does not exist in real life. In this guise B'Stard (or rather his creators, Laurence Marks and Maurice Gran) wrote a column for *The Daily Telegraph*, which allowed the appalling fellow to comment on Tony Blair's ups and downs.

'David' in *Love, Actually*

In the film by Richard Curtis, the prime minister (whose surname is never given) is played by Hugh Grant. The floppy-haired, charmingly stuttery Grant makes an unconvincing leader of a political movement, but verisimilitude has never been an integral part of Curtis's very successful recipe. In the film, we see the tentative beginnings of a romance between prime minister David and his attractive tea-lady Natalie (played by Martine McCutcheon).

There is an incident on screen in which Natalie is propositioned by the US president, and David publicly rebukes his American ally. This unlikely episode gave rise to a shortlived political expression 'the love-actually moment'. The term denoted the expectation that Gordon Brown, once installed as PM, would take a harder line with George Bush than Tony Blair had done. The love-actually moment never really came to pass, and the expression disappeared as suddenly as it had arisen. As for Blair, he is said to adore the film.

Ferdinand Lopez in
The Prime Minister

Anthony Trollope's eponymous hero is a thinly veiled caricature of Disraeli, whom Trollope despised. The apparently Spanish name of the PM hints at Disraeli's Sephardic Jewish ancestry. On the first page of the book, Trollope describes his hero's background in a way that would be openly anti-Semitic if it were just slightly more explicit: 'Ferdinand Lopez, who in other respects had much in his circumstances on which to congratulate himself, suffered trouble in his mind respecting his ancestors such as I have endeavoured to describe. He did not know very much himself, but what little he did know he kept altogether to himself. He had no father or mother, no uncle, aunt, brother or sister, no cousin even whom he could mention in a cursory way to his dearest friend.'

Terms of Office
The revolving door of Number Ten

Up to and including Boris Johnson, there have been 55 prime ministers since Robert Walpole, but 77 terms of office. That is to say, some prime ministers have had the job, lost it, then had it back again (a successive run of election wins, such as Thatcher's hat-trick, still only constitutes one term of office). Gladstone holds the all-time

Lord Salisbury

unbeatable record for terms of office with four separate terms. Lord Derby, Lord Salisbury and Stanley Baldwin each notched up an impressive three terms. Thirteen prime ministers have enjoyed two terms, among them some obscure ones such as the Marquess of Rockingham and the Duke of Portland, and also some well-known figures such as the Duke of Wellington, Lord Palmerston, Robert Peel, Benjamin Disraeli, Ramsay MacDonald, Winston Churchill and Harold Wilson.

Lord John Russell

Great and Small
The diminutive Lord John Russell

At five feet four inches, Lord John Russell was probably the shortest man ever to hold the office of prime minister. His small stature was the result of his premature arrival (he was born at seven months). His slight build, coupled with a weak constitution, troubled him deeply all his life.

Russell's first diary entry, written at Woburn in 1803, reads as follows: 'This is my birthday. I am eleven years old, 4 foot 2 inches high, and 3 stone 12 lbs weight.' Seven years later, aged eighteen and on the verge of manhood, his height was still evidently a concern to him. This can be inferred from a letter he received some months after leaving school. It was written to him by his good friend Lord Clare, who was almost as short as Russell himself: 'I am very much grown,' wrote the young Lord Clare, 'So I dare say are you. Don't be frightened; I am not yet a giant. *Entre nous*, I am only 5f. 6in. and a half. In your next letter tell me all about you, but don't forget your height.'

People who met Russell once he had become a political figure very often expressed surprise at how slight he was. But his smallness sometimes worked to his advantage. In some strange way, it made his skills as an orator and his energies as a reformer seem that much more impressive. One contemporary has left us a description of Russell speaking in the House. This was in 1838, before he became PM: 'In person diminutive and rickety, he reminded me of a pettifogging attorney. He wriggled around, played with his hat, and seemed unable to dispose of his hands or his feet; his voice was small and thin, but notwithstanding all this, a House of five hundred members was hushed to catch his smallest accents.'

Around the same time, Sydney Smith used Russell's smallness in order to big him up (as the modern expression goes). 'Before this reform agitation commenced Lord John was over six feet high,' joked Smith. 'But engaged in looking after your interests, fighting the peers, the landlords, and the rest of your natural enemies, he has been so constantly kept in hot water that he is boiled down to the proportions in which you now behold him.'

Born to Rule
Where do our prime ministers come from?

In the litany of British prime ministers there are three whose place of birth is not known. They are Devonshire, Grafton and Portland.

Of the remaining 52 PMs, the vast majority – 41 of them – were born in England. Eighteen of the Englishmen were Londoners. They are Newcastle, Devonshire, Pitt the Elder, North, Addington, Perceval, Liverpool, Canning, Goderich, Melbourne, Russell, Palmerston, Disraeli, Rosebery, Attlee, Macmillan, Douglas-Home, and Cameron.

Seven prime ministers have been born in Scotland, namely: Bute, Aberdeen, Balfour, Campbell-Bannerman, MacDonald, Blair and Brown. Two PMs were Irish-born: Shelburne and Wellington.

Two prime ministers hail from outside the United Kingdom. Andrew Bonar Law, who was born in Kingston (now known as Rexton),

The Duke of Wellington

in the province of New Brunswick, Canada. There is a school named after him in his home town. Boris Johnson is the only American born prime minister having been born in New York City.

Curiously, not one British prime minister has been born in Wales – not even David Lloyd George. The so-called 'Welsh wizard' was born in Manchester.

Speaking in Tongues
The Gladstones' private language

The Gladstones had an unusually close-knit extended family.

William had married Catherine Glynne in a double wedding; her younger sister Mary Glynne married Lord Lyttelton in the same ceremony in July 1839. The sisters were the best of friends, and spent much time in each others households.

Catherine had eight children with William (seven of whom survived infanthood); Mary had twelve with her husband. When Mary died young in 1857, Catherine took charge of her nephews and nieces as well as her own brood. So the Gladstone household had 19 children in all. No prime minister in history has had to contend with so many unruly and noisy distractions, if you discount the members of the parliamentary party.

Catherine Gladstone was as chaotic and untidy as her husband was neat and methodical – and unlike him she had a lively sense of humour. She once said to him, when he was holding forth on some matter of politics: 'Oh William, dear, if you weren't such a great man you would be a terrible bore.'

One manifestation of Catherine's wit was the strange private vocabulary that she invented. The Glynne sisters (and their children) called their domestic argot Glynnese, and among the colourful expressions that the family coined for their own use were: 'to troll', meaning to chatter; 'to show one's ring', which meant to be vain in a show-off way, like a newly betrothed woman with her engagement ring; 'pin-toed' – that is, feebly incapable of the kind of rough-and-tumble games that the family enjoyed.

Catherine Gladstone

Some Glynnese turns of phrase have the lively precision of Cockney rhyming slang: a 'moth', for example, was an old lady (wearing dusty grey lace, one imagines); a 'face' was an unexpected or uninvited dinner guest; 'grub' was not food, but news or gossip (as in 'Now, my dear, grub, grub...').

Some Glynnese words hint at the occasional tedium of life in the household of a professional politician. 'To be audience' meant to have to listen to someone drone on about their pet subject ('I was audience to his pony.') 'Powder-of-post' meant a pointless blizzard of written words (I had to write a powder-of-post letter...') The family believed that 'over the moon' for 'elated' was a piece of Glynnese. This seems unlikely given its universal currency today, but perhaps the Gladstones picked up the expression and made it their own while it still had some new life in it – before it died and became a cliché.

A number of Glynnese expressions were drawn from Greek or Latin. The name of the sorrowful nymph Niobe was used adjectivally to mean 'distraught' ('I was niobe', that is, 'I was in floods of tears'. The Latin word 'major' was used post-adjectivally as an intensifier, so a pleasing view might be described as 'lovely major'. For special emphasis the Latin superlative suffix could be added to English adjectives: 'The view was lovelyissimus major'.

This locution was twee in a way that only a bourgeois Victorian family could endorse, but there was worse. A particularly fruitful and favoured features of Glynnese morphology involved the plural suffix -ums in conjunction with the verb to have. So 'to have the churchums' meant to suffer, as if with a disease, from a dull and overbearing devotion to the outward forms of religion. William Gladstone, it might be said, 'suffered with a chronic case of the churchums all his life. He was also periodically struck down with another ailment first described by his wife and sister-in-law – a sickness known to them as 'the electionums'.

Words with Bite
Churchill's rhetorical false teeth

Churchill's speeches were a vital part of Britain's war effort, a kind of oratorical secret weapon. His resonant, growling voice and idiosyncratic diction were part of the special magic that he could weave with words.

But Churchill wore false teeth, like most men of his age and generation, and every time they were replaced there was a danger that something of his special vocal quality would be lost. Fortunately his dentist, a man named Cudlipp, was alive to the problem and deliberately designed his teeth to preserve Churchill's small speech impediment, his tendency to pronounce initial 's' sounds as 'sh-'. People were used to hearing the great Churchillian phrases with this oddity – "Never was sho much owed,

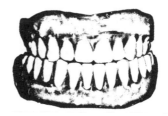

by sho many, to sho few…" – and it might have been damaging for public morale if a new set of dentures had put Churchill's problem right.

The Great Helmsman
Heath on the crest of a wave

In 1971 prime minister Edward Heath captained the British team to victory in the Admiral's Cup. This feat makes him the only premier

ever to participate in an international sporting event, let alone win it.

It says a great deal for Heath the sailor that he took up the sport a mere five years before his greatest moment of triumph. He had been a purely honorary member of the sailing club in Broadstairs until one day in 1966, an acquaintance suggested to him that it was about time he got out on the water. Heath replied 'I'll take you up on that,' and he very quickly became a skilled sea-going skipper.

Heath's yacht, Morning Cloud, turned out to be a longed-for escape from the political grind. 'He lived in a pressure cooker,' one of his crew members once said. 'I thought he was a bit of a lonely man. I know he had his politician friends, but we seemed to be a family to him. There was no politics on board, and whatever was said afloat never came ashore.' Though Westminster talk never went sailing, sailing talk often came to Westminster: 'We used to have long meetings at Number Ten when he became prime minister, to discuss how we could improve on our performances or the design of the boats.'

Within a year of Morning Cloud's maiden voyage, Heath steered his new yacht to victory in the Sydney to Hobart race across the Tasman Sea. But this was just a curtain-raiser for his real moment of glory: that Admiral's Cup race. In August 1971 Heath was at sea for five days, racing Morning Cloud II from Cowes on the Isle of Wight to Fastnet Rock on the south-western tip of Ireland, and back again.

Remarkably, Heath participated in the race – took a week's holiday, in effect – at a time of an intense political crisis. His government had laid plans to arrest IRA activists and hold them without trial; hundreds of suspects were rounded up in a massive operation that took place while Heath was away. The first days of internment set off a wave of deadly violence across Northern Ireland, and some newspapers suggested that perhaps the PM should be at his post in Downing Street. Government spokesmen disagreed: had Mr Heath changed his well-publicised plans, that alone might have alerted the IRA; and in any case he was being kept informed of developments via some

'very sophisticated radio equipment'. In addition to the cutting-edge radio, there was an emergency plan in place to set the prime minister adrift in a dinghy, so that he could be picked up by a navy helicopter without the yacht having to come to a stop, which might have endangered his team's chances of winning...

There were five Morning Clouds in all. Morning Cloud III was wrecked in freak waves off the Sussex coast in 1974, an incident in which Heath's godson was swept overboard to his death. Heath continued to sail, and took part in the Fastnet race in 1979 (by which time he was an ex-prime minister). In the course of that race 15 yachtsmen died, – a sad tally that affected Heath deeply, and must surely have opened an old emotional wound regarding his godson. He sold the fifth and final Morning Cloud in 1983, and gave up sailing altogether.

But the second Morning Cloud – the Admiral's Cup winner – limped on. It spent some years in Mediterranean waters, where it sustained damage and was subjected to some botched repairs. Eventually it was bought by someone who understood its historical significance. In 2008, the boat was brought to the Clare Lallow yard in Cowes and lovingly restored. Five of Heath's erstwhile crew gathered there for the relaunch of the yacht they had known so well and sailed in so memorably. As for Heath himself, he was not there – he had died three years earlier. And the name Morning Cloud was also no more; Heath's yacht was now called Opposition.

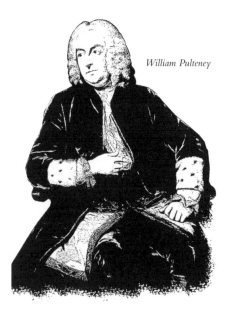

William Pulteney

A Quick Bath
William Pulteney's quite brief term of office

It is generally held that there have been 55 prime ministers of Britain, counting from Robert Walpole – the first man to hold the job in a recognisably modern form – to the latest incumbent, Boris Johnson. It is a well-known fact that Walpole set an unbeatable record for longevity right at the start by serving in the office of prime minister for a total of 20 years and 314 days. The shortest-serving prime minister is usually said to be Lord Canning, who continued in office for 119 days in all.

But there are two people who held the prime ministerial reins for such a short period that they are not included in the official lists at all. One of them is the Earl of Waldegrave who was First Lord of the Treasury for four rather unhappy days between the 8th and 12th of June 1757.

The other is William Pulteney, Earl of Bath, who – thirteen years before Waldegrave – headed the government for two days. His term of office began on February 10th, 1746, and came to an end around lunchtime on the 12th. Bath's time as prime minister was summed up at the time in a 'squib' entitled 'A History of the Long Administration'. The pamphlet ends with this splendid summation of his achievements:

'Thus endeth the second and last part of this Administration, which lasted forty-eight hours and three quarters, seven minutes, and eleven seconds; which may truly be called the most honest of all administrations; the minister to the astonishment of all wise men never transacted one rash thing; and, what is more marvellous, left as much money in the Treasury as he found in it…'

Dear Prime Minister
The growing postbag at Number Ten

Every citizen has the right to bring his or her grievances to the man (or woman) at the top, and there is a long democratic tradition in Britain of writing letters to the serving prime minister.

People write to complain about government policy, but also to offer advice and ideas, to air some local or personal issue, and occasionally just to heap threats on the highest political authority in the land (correspondents in this category usually get a visit from the police, if they are foolish enough to give their name and address). Every week brings sackfuls of harmless 'green-ink letters' – the scornful journalistic term for any kind of mad missive.

It was once possible for the prime minister to read his entire postbag, and even reply to every letter personally. Lord Grenville, who was prime minister at the beginning of the nineteenth century, received an entirely manageable sixty letters a week. Edward Heath in the 1970s would receive about 300 letters a week, many of which were answered, if they were answered at all, with a polite *pro forma*. The rise of computers and information technology has led to an exponential increase in the

volume of correspondence directed at Number Ten. Tony Blair at the height of his premiership received 7,500 letters each week. To deal with them personally, he would have had to have answered a letter a minute during all his waking hours, never taking a break or a day off, and of course never dealing with any other prime ministerial business at all.

THATCHER'S GATES

Downing Street is and always has been a cul-de-sac. But for most of its history it has also been a public road, and anyone who wanted to was free to stroll down and peep in the windows of Number Ten. That ceased to be the case in 1990, when Mrs Thatcher had a set of security gates erected at the Whitehall end. The rationale was that the free access represented too much of a security risk, but there were protests against the gates nevertheless. Somehow, they were seen not just as a physical barrier, but also as a symbolic divide between the governors and the governed, an ornate and unnecessary obstacle to open democracy.

Behind the Big Black Door
The power that resides at Number Ten Downing Street

Douglas Hurd, for many years a government minister under Margaret Thatcher, once said that 'Ten Downing Street is a house, not an office. And that is its most important characteristic.'

It is a remark that goes to the heart of the peculiar institution that is the prime minister's official HQ and residence. Because the fact is that in Britain the corridors of power are somewhat narrow and poky; many of the great decisions of state are taken not in a grand Oval Office or a presidential suite, but in the cramped downstairs rooms of a rather modest Georgian townhouse.

Douglas Hurd was perhaps also suggesting that the prime minister's view of the world is sometimes too narrow and cloistered as a result. It is surely no coincidence that past prime ministers have ended up presiding over a cosy 'kitchen cabinet' at Number Ten (Harold Wilson), or installing a jolly 'garden suburb' of typists and clerks out the back (David Lloyd George). Number Ten lends itself to this kind of cubby-hole domesticity. The obvious danger is that, in times of crisis, the insularity of the place can degenerate into a claustrophobic and paranoid bunker mentality.

One might characterise the bustle behind that black door by saying that it is akin to what goes on in a busy but rather ramshackle publishing house when it is on the point of outgrowing its unsuitable rented office space. Douglas Hurd hinted at the barely suppressed chaos that prevails inside Downing when he added that it is hard to imagine anything substantial being run from Number Ten.

So how did the prime minister – indeed a long succession of prime ministers – come to be in that particular house? What is the story behind Number Ten Downing Street?

The earliest building known to have stood on the site of Downing Street was a brewery known as The Axe. It had already stopped making beer by beginning of the reign of Elizabeth I, and the plot of land where the brewery stood was leased

by the queen to the keeper of the Palace of Westminster. This was the beginning of its connection with parliament. Some years later, the site passed into the possession of a relative of Oliver Cromwell's – which is another tenuous parliamentary link.

After the restoration of the monarchy in 1660, the land was acquired by George Downing, one of the Tellers of the Receipt of the

Exchequer. The young Samuel Pepys worked for George Downing, who merits several unflattering mentions in the early pages of his famous diary.

In 1680 Downing decided to build on his land as a speculative investment. A contemporary account says that Downing's new street consisted of 'four or five very large and well-built houses fit for persons of honour and quality.' Downing Street remained in private hands for about 50 years. Then, in 1732, the row of houses including Number Ten passed back into the possession of the Crown. King George II offered Number Ten to Robert Walpole, his chief minister. Walpole refused to accept it as a gift, but said that he would take the house in his official capacity as First Lord of the Treasury. So it was that Number Ten became the official residence of prime ministers almost at the beginning of the existence of that office.

But not all prime ministers have chosen to reside at No. 10. After Walpole, no prime minister occupied the house for 20 years. The Duke of Wellington lived there only until he was given a bigger house in Hyde Park. Sir Robert Peel lived elsewhere – a circumstance that saved his life when a deranged assassin named Daniel McNaughton shot a civil servant as he entered Downing Street, assuming the unfortunate man was Peel himself.

But all prime ministers since Balfour have lived and worked in Downing Street. In the 1930s, Neville Chamberlain and his wife adapted the rooms above Number Ten, and made them a more comfortable place to live.

The prime minister's flat is quite large as flats go – consisting of a drawing room and dining room along with six or seven bedrooms. But it was too small for Tony Blair and his family – especially once his family grew bigger. (Leo Blair, born in May 2000, was the first legitimate child to be born to a serving prime minister since 1849). So Blair arranged to swap flats with Gordon Brown, who as chancellor of the exchequer was entitled to live in the larger apartment next door. Brown thus became the only prime minister to live at Number Ten prior to getting the job that goes with it.

Inside Chequers
The country home of the ruling prime minister

A ll prime ministers are entitled to make use of Chequers, a country house near Aylesbury in Buckinghamshire, about 40 miles from Westminster. There has been a house on the site since the 12th century, but its history as a retreat for prime ministers is brief – far briefer than that of its urban counterpart in Downing Street.

In 1917 the owner of the house, Viscount Lee of Fareham, offered it to Lloyd George as a rural escape for the prime minister of the day. His thinking was that, in the democratic twentieth century, many a PM might come from too humble a background to have a country estate of his own, a place they could go to in order to get away the hurly-burly of parliament, and find some peace for a day or two.

Lloyd George happily accepted the viscount's offer, but did not make use of Chequers himself. Stanley Baldwin was fond of the place, as was Ramsay MacDonald. He would often sit reading for long hours beneath

Margaret Thatcher posing at Chequers alongside US President George Bush

the portraits of Oliver Cromwell (the house has an impressive collection of Cromwelliana).

Clement Attlee used the house often; Macmillan hardly at all since he had a country estate of his own, Lord Fareham's prophesy notwithstanding. Margaret Thatcher introduced her own housewifely sense of thrift to the place – totting up the cost of redoing the wallpaper, and insisting that the heating for the swimming pool be turned off.

Gordon Brown, when he came to power, had the intention of using the house not as a home, but as a kind of in-house think tank, a place to send his people for brain-storming sessions and working weekends. In the event, he used it in the traditional manner – as a bolthole for himself. Perhaps he did not realise how punishing his week's work would be, or how much he would need to get out of town and recharge his tired batteries.

CHEQUERS TREES

There is a strange tradition that every prime minister who visits Chequers plants a tree in the grounds to commemorate their time there. Most have chosen a species that is different from any selected by one of their predecessors. Margaret Thatcher planted a lime as her dendrological memorial: Callaghan a South American beech, Douglas-Home a walnut tree; Attlee a hornbeam; Eden a plane tree; Chamberlain an elm; MacDonald a cedar.

Unknown to Fame
Benjamin Disraeli, the London dandy

There are many reasons for wanting to be prime minister. An aspiring politician might be driven by a naked lust for power, by a sporting urge to defeat the opposition and win the game, by an idealistic longing to serve the nation, by a revolutionary's desire to alter or even destroy the political edifice – or by a subtle combination of such motives.

From a very young age, Benjamin Disraeli dreamed of reaching the top of the 'greasy pole' as he called it, and what he wanted above all was to be famous. 'I was devoured by ambition I did not see any means of gratifying,' he once said of his younger self.

Looking back from the vantage point of middle age, he said that he was 'full of energy and unknown to fame', though in fact the youthful Disraeli made a very early and impressive start towards notoriety. His first success was not in politics, however, but in literature. Disraeli published several novels in his early twenties, and looked set for a career as a writer. His perfumed early stories, almost unreadable today, are like Tolstoy's first works in one small respect: they all feature a central character who bears a more than passing resemblance to the writer himself. They are, in other words, a

series of egotistical self-portraits, 'the secret history of my feelings' as he later put it.

The problem with making a name for oneself as a writer, especially in the age before mass media, is that it is possible to be famous without actually being noticed. For Disraeli this was out of the question, and so he made sure that his manner of dress rendered him unmissable. Throughout his late teens and his twenties, Disraeli was an archetypal Regency dandy. At the age of nineteen he went out in 'a black velvet suit with ruffles, black stockings with red clocks'. He never grew tired of drawing attention to himself in this way, but some of his acquaintances thought his dandyism a very tiresome conceit. One wag said, punningly and anti-Semitically, that Disraeli was a 'Jew d'esprit'.

Such a jibe was never likely to deter a man as self-assured as Benjamin Disraeli. His friend William Meredith recalled seeing him on the streets of London one spring day in 1830, when the future prime minister was 26 years old. Meredith's description, as well as giving an account of Disraeli's dress, provides

A young Benjamin Disraeli

a clue to his highly affected way of speaking: 'He came up Regent Street, when it was crowded, in his blue surtout, a pair of military light blue trousers, black stockings with red stripes, and shoes. "The people," he said "quite made way for me as I passed. It was like the opening of the Red Sea, which I now perfectly believe from experience. Even well-dressed people stopped to look at me." I should think so!'

Later that year another friend noted that Disraeli had come to see him wearing 'green velvet trousers, a canary coloured waistcoat, low shoes, silver buckles, lace at his wrists, his hair in ringlets.'

Gaudy waistcoats were a particular affectation of Disraeli's, and he was rather put out when King George IV died and he had to refrain from wearing peacock colours during the period of mourning. The death of the king meant that he could not cut quite the dash that he wanted to, and he longed to be looked at. It seems incredible to us now (as it seems to have surprised him) that merely sporting two walking sticks in the course of a single day was enough

to do the trick. 'I have also the fame of being the first who has passed the Straits [of Gibraltar] with two canes, a morning cane and an evening cane. I change my cane as the gun fires, and hope to carry them both on to Cairo. It is wonderful the effect these magical wands produce. I owe to them even more attention than to being the supposed author of – what is it? – I forget!'

Horses for Courses
Lord Rosebery and the Epsom Derby

It is often said of Archibald Philip Primrose, Fifth Earl of Rosebery, that he claimed to have three ambitions in life: to marry an heiress, to own a horse that won the Derby, and to be prime minister. He was frequently asked about this remark and always replied that he never said anything of the sort. Maybe he didn't; maybe he did. But it is true that he achieved all three of the goals ascribed to him.

Lord Rosebery married Hannah Rothschild – heiress to a banking fortune – in 1878. He was 30 at the time. The couple were very happy together and, between them, almost inconceivably rich. That was the first of the imputed ambitions achieved.

The other two triumphs came later in life. The Derby win came as a particular surprise, since Lord Rosebery was a perfectly terrible judge of horseflesh. Over the course of his lifetime,

Rosebery's deep and abiding love of the turf cost him a fortune in rash bets and hopeless horses. One day in 1867, while he was an Oxford undergraduate, he lost the incredible sum of £1,698 in a single day's betting at Doncaster. Fortunately for him, he could afford it – even before he married his heiress.

It was around this time that he bought his first horse, a stallion named Ladas, which he was certain would be up to the job of winning the 1869 Derby. He was sadly mistaken: the bookmakers gave Ladas very long odds of 66:1, and to nobody's surprise it came in last.

Rosebery's luck as an owner improved over the years – possibly because he invested more money in the horses – but he did not achieve the longed-for Derby win until 1894. The horse in question was called Ladas II – the namesake of that first failure. That shared name ought not have augured well, but on the morning of the race Rosebery saw a hedgehog scurry speedily across the lawn of his house in Epsom; he recalled that on Derby Day in 1869 he had seen a dead hedgehog on that same lawn – and somehow that made the quick one seem like a good omen. Sure enough,

Ladas II romped home, to its owner's immense satisfaction. He even wrote a poem about the day that ended with the lines:

To bet may be unlawful
To race may be a sin
Still in racing, as in everything
It's always best to win.'

It must have seemed to Rosebery that 1894 was turning out to be a good year. After all, just a few weeks before his Derby win, Lord Rosebery had been appointed prime minister of England. It's always best to win.

Dizzy's Wit
Words of wisdom from the works of Benjamin Disraeli

Disraeli's narcissistic dandyism and precocious literary success are somewhat reminiscent of Oscar Wilde. And like Wilde, Disraeli was fond of peppering his works with breezy, cynical and pointed aphorisms. Here are some of those *aperçus*:

'Let me die eating ortolans to the sound of soft music.'

*

'The proof of the general dullness of polite circles is the great sensation that is always produced by a new face.'

*

'Something unpleasant is coming when men are anxious to tell the truth.'

'When you have been bored for an hour or two on earth, it sometimes is a change to be bored for an hour or two on water.'

★

'Unless we despise a woman when we cease to love her, we are still a slave.'

★

'Mankind are not more heartless because they are clothed in ermine; it is that their costume attracts us to their characters, and we stare because we find the prince or the peeress neither a conqueror nor a heroine.'

★

'A want of tact is worse than a want of virtue.'

★

'I rather like bad wine; one gets so bored with good wine.'

★

'It destroys one's nerves to be amiable every day to the same human being.'

★

'Youth is a blunder; Manhood a struggle; Old Age a regret.'

★

'An author who speaks about his own books is almost as bad as a mother who talks about her own children.'

Born for the Job
Robert Peel's pushy father

Robert Peel, twice prime minister in the early years of Queen Victoria's reign, came from a rich and influential family. His father, who was also named Robert Peel, owned cotton mills in Lancashire. The elder Peel was made a baronet in 1800 when he was 50 years old. He was also member of parliament for Tamworth – the same constituency that his son would later represent.

Robert Peel

It is to the credit of Robert Peel senior that he introduced to parliament the first ever legislation designed to protect child labourers in the mills. He may have been a capitalist – but he was, by the standards of his time, a caring and principled one. When his son Robert was born in 1788, the father fell on his knees and dedicated the boy to the service of his country. A few days later, at his christening, the elder Robert Peel confidently predicted that his son would one day follow in Pitt's footsteps.

Or so the story goes. It is possible that the prophesy ascribed to the first baronet, with its Old Testament overtones, are a sanitised version of a different anecdote, one that Robert Peel the younger often used to recount. One day, when Peel was a young man, his gruff father turned to him and said: 'Bob, you dog, if you are not prime minister some day I swear I will disinherit you.'

Top of the Greasy Pole
Prime ministers' reactions to getting the job

The manner in which a new prime minister goes about accepting the post can reveal a lot about his (or her) attitude to the premiership. Margaret Thatcher, for example, surprised everyone by quoting a prayer on the steps of Number Ten. 'I would just like to remember some words of St Francis of Assisi,' she said. 'Where there is discord, may we bring harmony. Where there is error, may we bring truth… And where there is despair, may we bring hope.' Historians will be kept busy for many years to come discussing the extent to which Thatcher succeeded in that aim.

Disraeli was predictably flippant when his call came, and at the same time characteristically smug. He told a friend that he had 'climbed to the top of the greasy pole at last'. A famous cartoon depicted him clinging to that pole for dear life. Gladstone, on being told that Queen's private secretary was on his way to ask him to form a government, murmured 'Very significant,' and carried on chopping down a tree.

Lord Melbourne was minded to refuse the premiership on the grounds that it was a 'damned bore'. His secretary, Ubiquity Young, took exception to the remark, saying: 'Why damn it? Such a position was never occupied by any Greek or Roman, and, if it lasts two months it is well worthwhile to have been prime minister of England.' Melbourne actually lasted considerably longer than that, but his seven years in office do not seem to have changed his initial opinion much. On being dismissed by William IV he said: 'I hardly ever felt so much relaxed or in better spirits in my life… nothing can be more delightful.'

In 1997, Tony Blair arranged to enter Number Ten via a corridor of cheering citizens (all of them carefully selected Labour party workers). It was a clever photo opportunity that made him look like a movie star working the red carpet at a film premiere. At an election celebration the previous evening he had declared 'A new dawn has broken, has it not?' It might be argued that the slightly narcissistic and messianic tone of Tony Blair's first hours in the job set the tone for his entire premiership.

Surely no prime minister has come to the premiership at a more fateful moment than did Winston Churchill. The country was at war, and it seemed highly likely that Britain would be invaded by Nazi armies within days or weeks. Churchill later wrote his own eloquent account of his feelings on that day, May 10th 1940. His reminiscence captures

the solemnity of the moment, and contains the faint glimmer of hope that sustained him and the nation through that darkest hour:

'I was conscious of a profound sense of relief,' he said. 'At last I had authority to give directions over the whole scene. I felt as if I were walking with destiny, and that all my life had been but a preparation for this hour and this trial… I was sure I should not fail. Therefore, although impatient for the morning, I slept soundly and had no need for cheering dreams.'

OUT OF THE HOUSE

Alec Douglas-Home is the only prime minister ever to hold the office while not being a member of either of the two houses of parliament. He became premier on October 19, 1963. He then resigned his peerage on the 23rd of the month with a view to fighting an easily winnable by-election at Kinross and West Perthshire on November 7th. So for fifteen days he was neither in the Lords, nor an MP in the Commons. For a fortnight he was, so to speak, constitutionally non-existent.

A KING'S NEW CLOTHES

Stanley Baldwin was prime minister at the time of the death of George V, and he was very worried that the Prince of Wales – King Edward VIII, as he became – would not make a suitable monarch. On the first day of the new reign Baldwin remarked to Attlee that he doubted the king would 'stay the course'. In the meantime, another future prime minister, Neville Chamberlain, produced a lengthy document full of ideas for making the flighty, pleasure-seeking king act in a manner that was more serious and becoming, more royal in fact. Among Chamberlain's suggestions was that the king should wear darker suits. None of Chamberlain's ideas, sartorial or otherwise, made any difference. Edward abdicated the throne within the year.

Sleepless in Mayfair
Lord Rosebery's cure for insomnia

Lord Rosebery was plagued with insomnia throughout his adult life, and the cares of high office made the problem worse. Throughout his short spell as prime minister, he had the haggard, wide-eyed look of a man who never enjoyed a good night's rest.

When his insomnia was very

Edward VIII

bad, Rosebery would have himself driven around London in his yellow carriage. (He once said that he found it amazing that no-one else made use of this marvellous cure: it did not occur to him that few people had a coach and horses that they could call on at any hour of the day or night.) The colour of Rosebery's conveyance was a reference to his family name: Primrose. Were it not for the cheery colour of his livery, the sight of him bowling through Mayfair in the small hours might have been rather sinister. And though these midnight jaunts relaxed him, they did not really solve his problem. The burden of office and the lack of sleep eventually brought on a nervous breakdown. Rosebery left office at the age of 47, and never took an active part in politics again.

Boardroom Bullies
Questionable behaviour in Cabinet

It is sometimes claimed that the British prime minister is constitutionally no more than *primus inter pares*, a first among equals. In the British system, so the theory goes,

the PM is like the chairman of a committee, whose job it is to garner the opinion of the other committee members (that is, the Cabinet), and then cook them down into policy. In reality, very few prime ministers have come close to this description, and many would consider it an utterly laughable ideal.

The Duke of Wellington, for example, came to the premiership after a lifetime of soldiering, and was rather bewildered by the attitude of

Lord Rosebery

his ministers. 'An extraordinary affair,' he said after his first Cabinet meeting. 'I gave them their orders and they wanted to stay and discuss them.'

This anecdote was recounted mirthlessly by members of Margaret Thatcher's cabinet after she first came to power. One of her ministers, Lord Soames, came out of her first Cabinet and said 'I wouldn't even treat my gamekeeper like that.' Mrs Thatcher justified her Wellingtonian approach by saying that 'as prime minister I could not waste time having internal arguments', and over the course of her premiership she tended to weed out ministers who dared to disagree with her.

Thatcher's perceived view of the cabinet as a kind of coterie of feckless errand boys was much satirised at the time, and was seen as a facet of her overbearing personality. But it can also be understood as part of gradual shift of political responsibility away from the political group (the ruling party, that party's MPs, or the Cabinet) towards the individual person of the prime minister. The slow concentration of power in the hands of an 'elected monarch' can be

said to have begun before Thatcher – Winston Churchill, had powers that were little short of dictatorial during the wartime coalition – and it's been a feature of more recent premierships. Tony Blair's style, for example, was unapologetically 'presidential'. Cabinet meetings under his leadership became briefer and more perfunctory than ever before. Important decisions were taken by Blair alone, or in consultation with his inner circle – only some of whom were government ministers or elected officials.

The Lib-Con alliance that emerged from the election of 2010 may yet mark a slowing-down of the drift towards presidentialism: it is hard for a PM to be crack down on dissent when part of his Cabinet owes its allegiance to a different party, and when he depends on that other party for his parliamentary majority.

Coalition government makes the Cabinet less biddable and bullyable. But coalition is a historically unusual and personally frustrating situation for a PM. And in the end, all prime ministers want the same thing: to get their own way.

Premier League

The 20th-century prime ministers ranked in order of greatness

In 1999, during the very last days of the millennium, *The Guardian* newspaper produced a league table of 20th-century prime ministers. The newspaper arrived at its rankings by collecting and collating the judgments of eminent historians, politicians and political journalists including Roy Jenkins, Barbara Castle, Kenneth Baker, Ben Pimlott and Andrew Roberts. The results of that straw poll are reproduced below.

1. Winston Churchill
(Conservative, 1940-45, 1951-55)
2. David Lloyd George
(Liberal, 1916-22)
3. Clement Attlee
(Labour, 1945-51)
4. Herbert Asquith
(Liberal, 1908-16)
5. Margaret Thatcher
(Conservative, 1979-90)
6. Harold Macmillan
(Conservative, 1957-63)
7. Marquess of Salisbury
(Conservative, 1895-1902)

8. Stanley Baldwin
(Conservative, 1923-24, 1924-29, 1935-37)
9. Henry Campbell-Bannerman
(Liberal, 1905-08)
10. Harold Wilson
(Labour, 1964-70, 1974-76)
11. Edward Heath
(Conservative, 1970-74)
12. James Callaghan
(Labour, 1976-79)
13. Andrew Bonar Law
(Conservative, 1922-23)
14. Ramsay MacDonald
(Labour, 1924, 1929-35)
15. Alec Douglas-Home
(Conservative, 1963-64)
16. Arthur Balfour
(Conservative, 1902-05)
17. John Major
(Conservative, 1990-97)
18. Neville Chamberlain
(Conservative, 1937-40)
19. Anthony Eden
(Conservative, 1955-57)

There were 20 prime ministers in the course of the twentieth century (Tony Blair was not included in the ratings, as he was only three years into his ten-year tenure at the turn of the century). The round total of 20 means that on average the premier served for five years. It is a neat coincidence that five years is the maximum term of a single parliament: it means that every prime minister has a right to expect one full term of office, that a second or third term is borrowed time.

It is notable in this regard that the prime ministers who served longest tended to come nearer the top of the rankings, and that those whose terms were shorter than average sank towards the bottom. Clearly it takes time for a PM to make a positive impression on posterity.

Another remarkable fact about

Anthony Eden

the list is that the most highly regarded five prime ministers were all, in a sense, war leaders – Churchill supremely so, and this is presumably the reason that he comes out top. Lloyd George successfully sold himself to the electorate as 'the man who won the war' (of 1914-18), and his self-assessment has become part of his historical reputation. Asquith led Britain into the First World War; Attlee led Britain out of the Second, and into a time of peace and reconstruction. Thatcher's conduct of the Falklands War gave her a huge popularity boost at the time, and certainly helped her win a second term in 1983. The two lowest ranking PMs, conversely, are both seen as war failures: Neville Chamberlain tried to avert it by appeasing Hitler; Anthony Eden mishandled it in Suez, which led to a humiliating defeat.

In 2004, the University of Leeds and the research organisation Ipsos Mori conducted a poll of 139 academics, asking them to rate the prime ministers of the twentieth century on a scale of one to ten. Tony Blair was included because, though he was still in office, the turn of the millennium was distant enough to provide some perspective on his performance in the 1990s. He came a creditable sixth. This time, Attlee pipped Churchill to the top spot – his achievement in presiding over the formation of the welfare state outdoing wartime leadership for once. Most of the PMs were within a place or two of their 1999 rankings, which suggests that the concensus of experts is slowly crystallising, and so becoming the judgment of history.

Be a Butcher and Know the Joints
Prime ministers on the cut and thrust of politics

Herbert Henry Asquith, PM from 1908 to 1916, once said that the 'office of prime minister is what its holder chooses and is able to make it'. And there is no doubt that differing prime ministers have had widely diverging views on the job – on its joys and its disappointments, and also on the rough and tumble of British politics.

Many prime ministers have felt that there is something slightly

immoral about the parliamentary sport in which they were the *de facto* reigning champion. Lord Rosebery observed that 'A gentleman will blithely do in politics what he would kick a man downstairs for doing in ordinary life.'

David Lloyd George might well have been the kind of gentleman Rosebery had in mind: 'If you want to succeed in politics,' he said, 'you must keep your conscience well under control.' Asquith thought that a politician's virtues were more important than his vices: 'In public politics as in private life, character is better than brains, and loyalty more valuable than either,' he said.

Many prime ministers have adhered to pithy rules of thumb for getting through the day unscathed. Melbourne's principle is the easiest to follow: 'When in doubt what should be done, do nothing'. Tony Blair's approach was almost as minimal: 'The art of leadership is saying no, not yes. It is very easy to say yes'.

Arthur Wellesley, the Duke of Wellington, always maintained that the tripartite secret of addressing the House of Commons was to 'say what you have to say, don't quote Latin, and sit down.'

Some of the best definitions of the role of prime minister have come not from people who have held the post, but from those have observed it at close quarters. RAB Butler, who was a contender for the job when Anthony Eden resigned in 1957, said that 'I think a prime minister has to be a butcher and know the joints. This is perhaps where I have not been quite competent, in knowing all the ways that you can cut up a carcass'. If that meat-hewing metaphor seems full of regret, then there is comfort to be taken in a remark attributed to Lord Hailsham (who was mooted as a successor to Macmillan in 1963). 'I've known every prime minister to a greater or lesser extent since Balfour,' said Hailsham, 'and most of them have died unhappy'.

Hailsham went on to serve as a minister in several governments, including Margaret Thatcher's. At the time, at least, she was very happy to have the job – delighted, in fact. She once described her occupancy of the post, with rather leaden humour, in the manner of a classified ad: 'Senior

position in government involving long hours, short holidays and tall orders. Expertise required in the whole range of government policy and especially in carrying cans. Tied cottage – makes job ideal for someone used to living above the shop. Current status: 650 applicants and no vacancy.'

Perhaps the most charming and noble definition of a prime minister's role was given by Stanley Baldwin. Soon after he became prime minister he made a broadcast to the British nation on the new-fangled wireless apparatus. In the course of that fireside chat he had this to say:

RAB Butler

'I am just one of yourselves, who has been called to special work for the country at this time. I never sought the office. I never planned out or schemed my life. I have but one idea, which was an idea that I inherited, and it was the idea of service, service to the people of this country. All my life I believed from my heart the words of Browning: "All service ranks the same with God". It makes very little difference whether a man is driving a tramcar or sweeping streets or being prime minister, if he only brings to that service everything that is in him and performs it for the sake of mankind.'

Cat, Cop, Club...
Ten things named after Mrs Thatcher

People in many fields of endeavour have been inspired to call some new thing after Britain's first female prime minister. Here are some of the unlikely things to bear the name of Mrs Thatcher:

• A red and white rose, and also an orchid (Ted Heath has a daffodil, Disraeli a fuchsia).

• The cat belonging to John Baird, Canada's minister of transport.

• A 80s-themed nightclub in Chelsea; it's called Maggie's.

• An optical illusion involving the unrecognisability of upside-down faces. It is called the 'Thatcher effect', and it was first demonstrated with a newspaper mugshot of Mrs T.

• Thatcherism – the only 'ism' to derive from the name of a British PM in the 20th century.

• One of a pair of Blue Peter tortoises (the other was called Jim, after James Callaghan).

• A character in the Canadian cop comedy-drama *Due South:* she was lightly disguised under the name of Inspector Meg Thatcher.

• A road in the Falklands: Margaret Thatcher Drive, Port Stanley.

• A method for calculating the margin of error in projected statistics. This mathematical device is known as 'Mrs Thatcher's Statistic', and its name is derived from her complaint that economists' lack of confidence in their own predictions 'leaves me breathless ... I sometimes wonder whether they back their forecasts with their money'.

Who's your Uncle?
How a helping hand can make all the difference

A rthur Balfour owed his start in politics to the help and encouragement of his uncle Robert Cecil, the marquess of Salisbury, who was prime minister three times between 1885 and 1902. It was Salisbury who leveraged his gifted but indolent nephew into the Commons by providing him with a safe seat in the election of 1874.

Balfour, 26 years old at the time, was returned to parliament unopposed. Two years later, Salisbury made sure that young Arthur got some real experience of foreign affairs by making Balfour his own private secretary and then taking him along to the Congress of Berlin. In 1885 Salisbury appointed Balfour President of the Local Government Board; the following year he promoted him to Secretary for Scotland, and gave him a seat in Cabinet.

In 1887, to the utter amazement of Westminster and the entire country, the rather ineffectual Balfour was made Chief Secretary for Ireland,

which at the time was the toughest, most punishing job in government.

Balfour turned out to be up to the task – one of his chief qualities was an ability to rise to a challenge. But there was no escaping the fact that it looked like favouritism. The expression 'Bob's your uncle' was coined around this time – a wry way of saying that friends in high places make almost anything possible. The association of the phrase with two prime ministers has faded over the years, and the nepotistic reproach has been lost. Now 'Bob's your uncle' is just a way of saying with a flourish that the path to one's goal is clear.

Arthur Balfour

Dictator or Democrat?
The two political faces of William Pitt

William Pitt, Earl of Chatham, is generally held to have been one of the greatest prime ministers – though he held office for barely two years in all.

But Chatham was by no means universally admired at the time. One contemporary said of him that: 'He is imperious, violent and implacable; impatient even of the slightest contradiction. Under the mask of patriotism, has the despotic spirit of a tyrant.'

This may have been true so far as Chatham's personal interactions were concerned. He had a dark temper, and could be foul to his subordinates. Like a kind of English Stalin, he frightened people – ministers included – into carrying out his wishes and orders. It was said that he personally wrote out orders for the navy, then made the First Lord of the Admiralty sign them without allowing him to read them. And he insisted on iron discipline and an almost regal formality in the office: his under-secretaries were never allowed to sit down in his presence.

But his autocratic manner notwithstanding, Chatham was a stout defender of traditional English freedoms, and of freedom in general. A couple of quotations will suffice to demonstrate that he was, at heart, a libertarian. Speaking of the rights of British subjects vis-à-vis the power of the state, he said:

William Pitt

'The poorest man may in his cottage bid defiance to all the forces of the Crown. It may be frail, its roof may shake, the wind may blow through it, the storm may enter, the rain may enter – but the King of England cannot enter! All his force dare not cross the threshold of the ruined tenement.'

More surprisingly, perhaps – because he was no supporter of the American cause – he had this to say on the American War of Independence when it was at its height: 'If I were an American, as I am an Englishman, while a foreign troop was landed in my country, I never would lay down my arms – never! never! never!'

THE QUIET ASSASSIN

David Lloyd George appointed Stanley Baldwin to his cabinet in 1921, little knowing that this quiet man would later oust him from office. In the eyes of the rest of the Cabinet, Baldwin was a pretty ineffectual colleague. Lloyd George himself complained the only sound he ever heard from Baldwin during meetings was the rhythmic sucking of his pipe. Perhaps those noises disguised an occasional tut-tut, because the effect on Baldwin of promotion to high government rank was a steady lowering of his opinion of the boss. Baldwin's gradual loss of respect for the prime minister is catalogued in his diaries. He wrote that Lloyd George the prime minister had a 'disintegrating effect on all with whom he had to deal', and that he is 'a real corrupter of public life'.

Constabulary Work to be Done
Sir Robert Peel and the invention of the police

It is generally agreed that Sir Robert Peel was one of the great reforming prime ministers. He transformed the administration of crime and punishment in Britain, and in almost every respect the changes were for the better.

Peel overhauled the prison system, for example. He also ensured that the death penalty, when it had to be applied, was administered consistently, and in respect of a greatly reduced list of crimes. Peel revamped the jury system, and he introduced legal changes to sweep away the tangled mess of medieval laws and statutes that defined British justice well into the nineteenth century.

The achievement for which Peel is best remembered was part of this general renewal in the sphere of law and order. When he was Home Secretary, Robert Peel introduced the Metropolitan Police Improvement Bill, which made provision for a professional, uniformed police force in London.

Peel was not the first prime minister to attempt to do this. Pitt the Younger had tried to pass such a bill in 1785, but his proposal was defeated in parliament. English MPs, and Englishmen in general, had an aversion to the idea of a body of uniformed men under the control of the government, because it raised memories of Cromwell's armed dictatorship. This British distaste for police organisations was reinforced by the rise of Napoleon. That great dictator had instituted a national police in France, and to English

minds the regiments of *gendarmes* on the streets of Paris were an obvious and highly visible aspect of his Continental brand of tyranny.

But the streets of British cities were increasingly lawless, and by the 1820s it was becoming clear that some kind of law enforcement was necessary. In 1822 Peel chaired a committee to look into the question; it concluded that the concept of a police force was irreconcilable with a free society. But Peel did not give up. He returned to the idea in 1828, proposing a committee of enquiry into crime in London. This time, the committee came down on Peel's side, and recommended the institution of a police force.

Peel's police bill was passed in the summer of 1829. In the years to come, a series of police acts followed, whereby one city after another set up its own police force. The fact that they were locally recruited, and paid for by the locality, went a long way to allaying fears of a national paramilitary force at the beck and call of the government. That parochial infrastructure also accounts for the fact that in modern Britain, each police force is an autonomous organisation. There is still no national police. Instead there is the Durham Constabulary, Thames Valley Police, and also long-standing anomalies such as the tiny City of London Police, a completely separate force from the Metropolitan Police, with jurisdiction just over the Square Mile. Even the uniforms of policemen differ from town to town. If you know what to look for, you can tell a Glaswegian copper from a Liverpudlian one just by his dress, in particular by the shape of the helmet and the crest on the front of it.

The uniform worn by the first London policemen was part of Peel's strategy to sell the idea of a professional force to the British public. It was deliberately unmilitary and, Peel hoped, it looked non-threatening to law-abiding citizens. The constables wore dark blue serge (not army red), and they sported top hats that were more or less civilian. But concealed in the tails of their coats was a truncheon, along with a loud rattle for attracting the attention of fellow officers.

The first London policemen went on duty on September 29th, 1829. They were not an immediate success. The man issued with warrant No.1 was dismissed four hours into his law-enforcement career for being drunk on duty. Most of that first batch of policemen were subsequently sacked for one professional misdemeanour or another. But these teething problems were not enough to kill off the force: the Metropolitan Police grew and took root in society.

Police constables were called 'Peelers' in Ireland (Peel had for six

turbulent years been Chief Secretary for Ireland), but that nickname never really caught among the English. In London, the constables became known as 'bobbies' – a term which, like 'peeler', was a reference to the name of the man who founded the force. 'The bobby on the beat' is Peel's legacy to the English language, and to England's civil structure.

Neville Chamberlain

FLYING VISIT

In 1938, when prime minister Neville Chamberlain made his famous flight to Munich to meet Adolf Hitler, it was the first time he had even been on an aeroplane.

Thatcher the Compassionate
The soft side of the Iron Lady

Margaret Thatcher was often seen as unfeminine, even uncaring. The satirical puppet show *Spitting Image* took to depicting her in a man's suit, snarling sarcastically at her cabinet of men. And in life, her blonde coiffure looked as fixed and undentable as a jouster's helmet. And like the knights of old, she always seemed on the point of launching into the attack. As the Conservative MP Julian Critchley once quipped: 'She can't see an institution without hitting it with her handbag.'

But Mrs Thatcher did have an emotional side. It was well hidden, and the nation was always surprised when it showed through. Thatcher cried publicly when her son Mark went missing for several days while taking part in a car rally in the Sahara. And she had tears in her eyes again on the day that she was ousted from power, and left Downing Street for the last time.

There is also the telling story of an incident that occurred early in her term of office. She was hosting a dinner at Chequers for senior members of government, and when the main course was served, the waitress tripped and spilled a plateful of stew into the lap of Geoffrey Howe, the foreign minister. He was not pleased; and as for the waitress, she was utterly mortified. But Mrs Thatcher jumped up from her chair and rushed over to her. She put her arm round the girl and said: 'Don't worry, my dear, it could happen to anyone.'

This was an almost regal act of kindness and, decades later, it must still warm the cockles of that waitress's heart to think of it.

Margaret Thatcher

Out the Door
Becoming an ex-PM

Most prime ministers find it hard to look kindly on their successors; that is just human nature. A PM at the point of leaving office is usually a failure by definition – because he has just lost an election or been ousted by his (or her) own party. A new prime minister is, by the same token, always a winner, because all his mistakes are still in the future. That is hard for the loser to take.

Edward Heath, for example, spent so much time fulminating against his successor as party leader, Mrs Thatcher, that his attitude to her began to be described as 'the longest sulk in history'. Tony Blair was monumentally ungracious towards Gordon Brown, describing his old friend in his memoirs as a man who lacked political instinct, had 'zero emotional intelligence' and was guilty of 'constant obstruction and wilful blocking'.

It is interesting to note that both Heath and Blair saved their harshest words for successors who belonged to the same party – and that too is human nature. It is far easier to forgive your enemies than your allies. Labour PM Tony Blair always treated Conservative Margaret Thatcher with kindness and respect, and Clement Attlee never held Winston Churchill in anything but the highest esteem.

Most prime ministers have numerous successors in the course of their own lifetime – and perhaps, with time and age, it gets easier for an ex-premier to see younger people take the reins. The prime minister who lived to see the largest number of PMs step into his shoes was Henry Addington. He occupied the post from 1801 to 1804, before he died thirty years later in 1844. In that time he saw nine other men do the job: Lord Grenville, Spencer Perceval, the Earl of Liverpool, George Canning, Goderich, Wellington, Earl Grey, Melbourne and Peel. It is doubtful, in our politically more stable age, that any

prime minister will beat that record. The average term of office for a prime minister over the past 60 years or so (from Macmillan to May inclusive) has been approximately five years two months. It is generally accepted that the shortest-serving prime minister is Lord Canning at 119 days, and although the last 60 years have been politically stable, the current political climate would suggest that this record could be easily beaten.

Lend me your Ear
Wellington's unlikely brush with an untimely death

In 1822 the Duke of Wellington noticed that he was growing increasingly hard of hearing. He decided to allow a quack physician by the name of Mr Stephenson to syringe his ears with a solution of caustic. 'I don't think that I ever suffered so much in my life,' said Wellington, the veteran of many battles. 'It was not pain; it was something far worse. The sense of hearing became so acute that I wished myself stone deaf. The noise of a carriage passing along the street was like the loudest thunder, and everybody that spoke seemed to be shrieking at the top of his voice.'

The treatment had an unsettling effect on Wellington's balance for a while. His personal doctor Hume saw him the day after Stephenson's administrations and found him reeling like a drunk. And despite what Wellington said about his newly sharpened hearing, the treatment left him completely deaf in one ear.

Doctor Hume took the view that a second syringeing, as recommended by Stephenson, would have finished

Herbert Henry Asquith

Wellington off altogether. That would have been a very peculiar end for the hero of Waterloo.

Speak Easy
Asquith's gift of the gab

Herbert Henry Asquith regularly alarmed his aides by standing up to make a speech apparently without having made any preparation whatsoever. But their fears were never realised, since he had the gift for speaking eloquently and at considerable length with few notes.

The story goes that Asquith once gave a speech at a public meeting on the subject of the Licensing Bill. He spoke long and well, though temperance was not a cause he readily espoused (Bonar Law once said that 'he can make a better speech drunk that the rest of us can sober'). At the end of the evening a lady approached him to ask if she could have his notes as a memento of his fine performance. 'Certainly,' said Asquith, and pulled from his waistcoat a small scrap of paper on which was written the single phrase: 'Too many pubs.'

NORTH'S NAP

Lord North liked to have a snooze on the benches of the House of Commons. Or rather he pretended to do so – either as a comment on the rhetoric of a fellow member, or as a means of avoiding taking part in the debate. There was one occasion when a speaker stopped mid-flow to complain that the prime minister was fast asleep. North opened his eyes and said 'I wish to God I were.'

Pam's Scandals
Digging the dirt on Lord Palmerston

Sex and politics are a combustible mix. Even before our tabloid age, a fruity scandal had the power to blow a career sky high. Once, when Benjamin Disraeli was leader of the opposition, he was approached by a shadowy figure named Spofforth, who told him that he had important information about Lord Palmerston, then the very elderly prime minister. Disraeli agreed to meet Spofforth in the presence of his secretary, Monty Corry. Spofforth informed Disraeli

that Palmerston was having an affair with a married woman, and that he had given a post to the woman's husband as a kind of sop to his feelings. Spofforth felt that if the facts came out, the government would fall.

Disraeli's reaction was not what Spofforth had hoped. He said that if a word of the affair found its way into the newspapers then he would resign his leadership of the Conservative party instantly. Then he turned to Corry and added 'My dear Monty, if it became known that Palmerston had a liaison at eighty, the English people would make him dictator.'

Lord Palmerston

The Pursuit of Idleness
*The slothful philosophy of
Arthur Balfour*

It is generally agreed that Arthur Balfour was the laziest prime minister ever to hold office. Even as a boy he was markedly indolent. When he was ten years old, his school report described him as 'lacking in vital energy'. While other boys were playing games in the afternoons, he would go for a lie-down and listen

Arthur Balfour

to the sound of organ music wafting from the school chapel.

As prime minister he did all he could to avoid reading newspapers or government documents. His staff had to beg him to cast an eye over important memoranda or articles. He much preferred lighter stuff, and he always read a chapter or two of a cowboy novel before bedtime. He got up late most days, and right through his political career he took a month off every year solely to play golf.

There was a distinctly lethargic element to Balfour's philosophy of life which he summed up, rather brilliantly, in these words: 'Nothing matters very much, and very few things matter at all.'

Like Father...
*Political dynasties in the
House of Commons*

Two sons of prime ministers have followed in their political footsteps all the way to the highest office in the land.

William Pitt the Elder, prime minister from 1766 to 1768, was (naturally enough) the father of

William Pitt the Younger, prime minister from 1783 to 1801, and then from 1804 to 1806. Less famously, George Grenville, prime minister from 1763 to 1765, was the father of Lord William Wyndam Grenville, who held the job from 1806 to 1807 – taking over the post from the younger Pitt. Intriguingly, the Pitts and the Grenvilles were part of the same extended family. The younger Grenville was married to Anne Pitt, who was the niece of the Elder and the cousin of the Younger.

In modern times, no son (or daughter) has trailed a father (or mother) as far as Downing Street, though plenty of prime-ministerial offspring made it to the House of Commons. Churchill, Macmillan, Bonar Law, Russell and Lloyd George all had sons in the Commons. Three of Lord Aberdeen's boys became members of parliament, and so did three of Peel's. The record holder as regards PMs begetting MPs, is held by the Earl of Bute: four of his five sons had seats in the House.

Oliver Baldwin, son of Stanley, is an interesting case because he ran as a Labour candidate in the 1924 election, when his father was the Conservative prime minister. The fact that his son opposed him was something of an embarrassment for Baldwin, especially since Oliver was fond of making personal attacks on Stanley. Oliver was elected, and duly took his seat in parliament. From that time on his mother, Baldwin's wife Lucy, could never bring herself to attend the House: she found it too painful to see father and son seated on opposing benches. Stanley and Oliver had a difficult relationship even apart from their political opposition to each other. But in a rare conciliatory moment, when the 1924 election was over, Oliver told his father that 'I have never heard any of our [Labour] supporters speak other than in a kindly way of your personal self.'

SNIFFY STAN

Baldwin was an inveterate sniffer of books. It was a rather unappealing nervous habit that stayed with him all his life, and became more pronounced in old age. In his last years he spent a great deal of time with his nose in the many dusty volumes in his library – not reading, just smelling. He continually sniffed at other things too, especially when he was lost in thought: spent matches, the bowl of his pipe, inkpots and the other paraphernalia of a busy desk – always with audibly ingressive snort of the nostrils.

Lord North

Ugly Rumours
Lord North, his wife and his daughter

L ord North was once attending a performance at Covent Garden, when he was approached in his box by a slight acquaintance. The two men spoke superficially for a while, and then the visitor asked: 'Who is that plain-looking woman in the box opposite.'

'That is my wife,' replied North amiably.

'No, no,' said North's companion, casting round for a way to save face. 'I meant the dreadful monster sitting next to her.'

'That, sir, is my daughter,' replied North. 'We are considered to be three of the ugliest people in London.'

The incident became very well known in political circles at the time, and has been retold ever since. Viscount Goderich, possibly the most obscure prime minister of them all, once related this tale at dinner to the lady seated next to him. After he delivered the punch line she said to him. 'I know that story. I am Lord North's wife'.

More Ugly Rumours
*Tony Blair's mercifully brief
Mick Jagger phase*

Before Tony Blair went into law, and subsequently into politics, he had a punt at a career in popular music. First he tried his hand as an impresario. Then, once he arrived at university, he briefly fronted a band. By all accounts, Tony the rock star was supremely self-confident, possessed of a rather bumptious charm, and desperate to be popular – not unlike Tony the prime minister.

Blair's flirtation with the music industry began at school in Scotland, where he was known to have something of an obsession with Mick Jagger. His schoolmates recall that he could do a very convincing Jagger impression – complete with struts, pouts and waving arms. When Blair left school he took a gap year before he went to university. He came down from Edinburgh to London with an old suitcase and a homemade blue guitar that he referred to gigglingly as 'Clarence'.

Blair turned up on the Kensington doorstep of a friend of a friend, Alan Collenette. He too had just left school, and was planning to become a rock promoter. Blair announced that he was a guitarist, just the kind of person that Collenette might like to handle. He added that he could really use a bed for the night. Collenette was persuaded, and took Blair in. He asked his new flatmate to audition for him. It turned out that Blair knew only two chords – and no sooner had he played them both than the neck fell off his guitar. Blair saw that he did not make a convincing axe hero, and suggested shrewdly that he help Alan on the organisational side of things. This was the start of Blair-Collenette Promotions (Tony insisted that his name go first).

Tony and Alan arranged a series of gigs for amateur bands in church halls, but this was small-time stuff. Blair had an idea to put himself on the map by booking a professional band to play at a large venue. He booked a concert hall, then rang up the management of Free, at the time one of Britain's biggest blues-rock groups. Blair was told that Free would expect to be paid £25,000 for the gig – many times more money that he was expecting to make on ticket sales. He later remarked that 'Free don't come cheap,' – which was probably the nearest thing to a good joke that he ever uttered.

Blair abandoned the promotions business when he went to Oxford to begin his legal studies. But at university, the performer in Blair came back to the fore. He took part in student revues, where his talent for holding the gaze of a crowd was noticed and widely remarked upon. He came to the attention of a young musician named Mark Ellen (subsequently a well-known music journalist), who was putting together a band and was in need of a front man. The band was called Ugly Rumours, and Blair was invited to do his Jagger turn once more as its lead singer. It is now impossible to say whether the band was any good or not – almost certainly not, because no student band is. But for one reason or another Ugly Rumours played only a handful of gigs, and then called it a day. Tony buckled down to his studies, and gradually became involved in left-wing politics...

But he never entirely gave up on music. Somewhere along the way he acquired a new guitar, one that didn't fall apart after ten seconds' strumming. During his years in power he was often seen carrying a guitar case when setting off for a holiday or a working weekend at Chequers. He also learned a few more chords. Alastair Campbell, Blair's press secretary, has said that the prime minister would often be trying out some new riff or chord sequence when, late at night, they would be talking on the phone about the war in Iraq.

And Tony continued to be slightly in awe of genuine rock musicians. Oasis frontman Noel Gallagher was one of the first celebrities that he invited to a Downing Street reception. This was in the days when Brit pop and 'cool Britannia' seemed somehow to be part of the same vibrant, vivacious upsurge of national pride as New Labour. Blair clearly identified with people such as Gallagher, who had achieved the kind of fame that he had hankered after in his youth. He never did get to be a rock star, but he was perhaps the first and only rock'n'roll prime minister.

WHAT'S IN THE NAME

The name of Tony Blair's group, Ugly Rumours, was a little homage to the American band Grateful Dead. The band's seventh album, Grateful Dead from the Mars Hotel, had just been released when Mark Ellen was putting together the band. On the cover of the album is a surrealist picture of a tall building in a starlit moonscape. Hold the album upside down to a mirror, and it becomes clear that the stars spell out the words 'ugly rumors', spelled after the American fashion. This knowing reference appealed to Ellen, who was an ardent 'Dead Head'.

Beware the Iron Lady
The Russians' accidental compliment to Mrs Thatcher

Many prime ministers have been known by nicknames – positive ones, insulting ones, ironical ones. Pitt the Elder was 'The Great Commoner', Gladstone, the 'Grand Old Man' or 'GOM'. Earl Russell was known as 'Finality Jack' (which makes him sound like a small-time Chicago gangster), Asquith was 'Squiffy', the Earl of Derby was 'Scorpion Stanley', and Balfour – troublingly – was referred to as 'Pretty Fanny'.

Tony Blair's winsomeness earned him the occasional sobriquet of 'Bambi', and Mrs Thatcher, when she abolished the provision of free milk for school children, was endowed with the hostile rhyming epithet 'Milk Snatcher'. This was in the mid-1970s, before she became prime minister. Around the same time that she acquired another nickname, one she grew into over the next decade and a half: 'the Iron Lady'.

Bizarre as it may seem, the nickname Iron Lady was coined by the Soviets, specifically by a Russian military journalist whose name was Yuri Gavrilov.

In January 1976 Gavrilov was working as a sub-editor for the Soviet Army newspaper *Red Star*. The paper was running an angry article about a speech that Thatcher had made in parliament, in which she said that the 'Russians are striving for world domination'. Gavrilov wrote the headline 'Iron Lady Raises Fears' for the piece. He said much later that he intended a reference to Otto von Bismarck, Germany's belligerent 19th-century leader, who was known as the 'Iron Chancellor'. To a Brezhnev-era Soviet mind, that was hardly a flattering comparison. But Gavrilov thought no more of it at the time. *Red Star* went to press, and the Iron Lady epithet duly appeared in print the next day.

And that would have been the end of it – two words in an obscure foreign paper – had not *The Sunday Times* picked up on Gavrilov's lively coinage and brought it to the attention of the British public the following weekend. The term immediately caught on, partly because it was neatly ambiguous:

to Thatcher's detractors – the ones who called her Milk Snatcher – it spoke of intransigence and a hard heart; to her supporters it suggested a steely purpose and strength of will. Somehow, obscurely, the name alone served to increase Thatcher's standing at home and abroad, and the Tories were canny enough to make use of it in the 1979 election: 'Britain needs an Iron Lady,' they claimed.

In the years that followed, even the Russians came to use it as a term of respect – and all the more so when Thatcher opposed Soviet actions in Afghanistan and elsewhere. Thatcher, evidently, was a strong leader of a kind that generations of Russians knew and understood. When she came as prime minister to Moscow for talks with Mikhail Gorbachev, all the Soviet state media noted approvingly that she wore elegant but skimpy high-heel shoes while standing in the snow and ice of a sub-zero Moscow winter –and never showed the slightest sign of feeling the cold. The Iron Lady, it seemed, had iron toes.

Interestingly, the Russians subtly changed the 'Iron Lady' nickname to reflect the evolving political reality. Yuri Gavrilov's original headline had used the Russian word *dama* for lady; a merely polite term for a bourgeois Western housewife. Later, Soviet commentators started to use the transliterated English term *leidi*, which to a Russian ear has deferential, upper-class overtones. The iron woman had somehow floated up the social scale and become an iron duchess. By this time, 20 years after the original *Red Star* article and well into the era of *glasnost*, that was a definite accolade.

As for Gavrilov, he now claims that he only ever intended a compliment. 'I always found her attractive as a woman,' he said. 'If I hadn't, maybe I would have used a harsher label to describe her. She was possessed with a kind of aristocratic beauty. And he added: 'The Queen made you a baroness, and that is a high title, but there are many baronesses around. The title I awarded you is unique. And you are the only one in history who deserves it.'

Brothers in Office
The premierships of Pelham and Newcastle

In the autumn of 2010, Britain watched with fascination as two brothers – David and Ed Miliband – fought for leadership of the Labour Party, both of them hoping one day to be prime minister. Ed won, and David's political career collapsed around his ears. But there is no reason to think that two brothers cannot both aspire to lead the country. It has

Thomas Pelham

happened before – and as with the Milibands, it was the younger brother who made the running.

Henry Pelham was the second son of the Duke of Newcastle. He became a member of parliament at the age of 23, and a minister at 26. He served for many years under Robert Walpole, who was his good friend.

Henry's elder brother Thomas was also one of Walpole's inner circle – though his relations with the prime minister were sometimes strained. Henry sat in the House of Commons as MP for Sussex; Thomas, who inherited the dukedom at the age of 19, was never an MP: he sat in the House of Lords.

When Walpole resigned the premiership in 1742, his post was offered to Henry Pelham. He turned it down out of loyalty to Walpole, and the job went instead to Spencer Compton, Earl of Wilmington. But Compton did not think he was up to the task, and most people agreed with him. One contemporary wrote that he was 'a plodding, heavy fellow with great application but no talents…'

Wilmington served as prime minister for a year and a half, during which time he achieved very little. He died suddenly in office in 1743.

The premiership was once again offered to Henry Pelham, and this time there was no reason not to accept. The younger Pelham turned out to be very good at the job. He was blessed with an ability, rare among politicians, of being able to unite people of differing views in a common cause. He created what might these days be called 'a government of all the talents' an administration that encompassed both Whigs and Tories. At the time this arrangement was termed 'the broad-bottomed ministry' – a name which also contained a disrespectful reference to the prime minister's own generous behind.

Henry's elder brother – the Duke of Newcastle – served under Henry, and was his main confidant even though the siblings often quarrelled about matters of policy. Pelham's premiership lasted for more than ten years, during which the Jacobite rebellion in Scotland was quelled, and the War of Austrian Succession was brought to a peaceful conclusion. Pelham was seen as a peacemaker in every sense – and this was much to his credit. But his time in office came to an abrupt end. In March 1754 he went for a walk in St James's Park, caught a chill, and (like his predecessor) very suddenly died.

It was the eve of a general election, and the awkward political situation at the time of the prime minister's death made it easy for the Duke of Newcastle to step into his deceased brother's shoes. Some said at the time that he was a little too eager to take over the government, but there is every reason to believe that Newcastle was genuinely distraught by the manner of his accession. 'I have the greatest loss that man can have,' he wrote at the time, 'and now have no view but to endeavour to pursue his measures, serve his friends, and particularly to do everything that can best comfort his family… I have no comfort so great as that of following my dearest brother's example… and go to the head of the Treasury.'

Newcastle served two terms – the first lasting for less than two years, the second nearly five – during which Britain was almost constantly at war with France.

NOW READ THE BOOK…

Many prime ministers have published books before or after leaving office. Generally these are memoirs or autobiographies (Disraeli is unique in that he was a novelist). Rosebery and Churchill both wrote very readable history. Churchill has the distinction of being the only prime minister to win a Nobel Prize for Literature, which he received in 1953, during his last term of office. To the end of his days, he remained slightly annoyed that he was not subsequently awarded a Nobel Peace Prize too: he rather thought he had earned it.

Sex and the City of Westminster
Unparliamentary liaisons

Many prime ministers have conducted extra-marital affairs. Lord Palmerston was a notorious womaniser, and Lloyd George's disparaging nickname, 'the Goat', was in part a reference to his well-known promiscuity. His most serious affair was with his secretary

Frances Stevenson, a schoolmate of his daughter's. Stevenson became Lloyd George's personal secretary in 1913, and eventually settled into such a domesticated life with him that she in effect became his London wife. His actual wife, Margaret, remained in Wales, where she looked after constituency business.

Edwina Currie

By far the most astonishing prime-ministerial love affair of modern times was the entirely secret *amour fou* that took place between John Major and Edwina Currie. He was then a government whip, and she a very media-savvy backbencher. Their affair

lasted four years, between 1984 and 1988, but no hint of it emerged at the time, or during Major's premiership. Perhaps the hints were there in the parliamentary bonkbusters that Currie began to churn out towards the end of the Conservative regime, but the far more interesting true story did not come to light until 2002, when Currie published her diaries. Here she described their late-night trysts, which included long discussions about what government post Currie might aspire to. She seems to have wanted something that would get her close to Major, and also place her at the hub of government. After the 1992 election Major offered her the post of prisons minister; she turned it down, saying later that it was a 'crap job'.

But this professional snub was not what made Currie decide to make the long-dead affair public. It seems that the key thing for her was the publication of Major's memoirs, in which she did not get a single mention, not even in the index. This erasure of the place she had occupied in his life was, as she saw it, an unbearable lie of omission. By making the affair the centrepiece of her own memoir she could claim to have set the historical record straight. And, of course, she guaranteed maximum publicity for her own book.

Currie completed her revenge by detailing small but embarrassing details of their liaison, related in her eye-watering prose. In one much-quoted passage, she declares: 'I wish my flat was filled with one big man in his blue underpants'.

OLD BOYS' NETWORK

Stanley Baldwin was very fond of trains. He studied timetables for fun, and travelled on trains alone even after he became prime minister (an unthinkable luxury for a modern-day PM). On one occasion, during his second term of office, he was in a train carriage when he noticed that another passenger was looking at him strangely. After a while the stranger leant forward and said 'You are Baldwin, aren't you?' Baldwin said that he was. 'Weren't you at Harrow in '84?' 'Yes,' said Baldwin, 'I was.' The chap that Baldwin now knew to be a fellow Harrovian seemed satisfied, and there was a pause in the conversation. Then the man tapped Baldwin on the knee again and said: 'So tell me, Baldwin, what are you doing these days?'

Before a Fall
Prime ministers and their bumps, hurts and scrapes

A surprising number of prime ministers have had nasty accidents of one sort or another. Gladstone lost the top joint of one finger when a gun that he was loading exploded in his hand. John Major had a bad car accident in Nigeria when he was a young man: he badly damaged his knee, and the injury put an end to his cricket-playing days. MacDonald was once bumped off his feet by a man on a bicycle, and Macmillan was knocked down by a taxi.

The Earl of Bute, when in his seventies, fell off a ten-metre-high cliff while collecting plants near his home in Hampshire; Gordon Brown

lost the sight in his left eye at sixteen as the result of an injury sustained while playing rugby.

In 1838, Earl Grey was nearly killed when a portrait of his wife fell off the wall onto his head; he was bedridden for a month. Sir Robert Peel, like Gladstone, hurt himself while shooting: a cartridge exploded near his ear, leaving him partially deaf and suffering from chronic tinnitus.

Years later Peel fell from his horse while out riding on Constitution Hill. The horse fell on top of him, making bad injuries worse. This mishap was the end of him: he died at home three days later.

FELLOW AMERICANS...

During the American War of Independence, Lord North made a speech at a dinner in which he referred to colonists as 'rebels'. The radical politician Charles James Fox, who supported the revolutionary cause, objected to the use of such a term for 'our fellow-subjects in America'. 'Very well, then,' said North wearily. 'I will call them "the gentlemen in opposition on the other side of the water."'

An Unknown PM
The unjust eclipse of Andrew Bonar Law

Andrew Bonar Law had the shortest term of any 20th-century prime minister. He held the post for 209 days, before retiring through ill health. He had cancer of the throat, and died soon after leaving office, in 1923.

At Bonar Law's funeral in Westminster Abbey, Asquith is said to have remarked: 'It is fitting that

Andrew Bonar Law

we have buried the Unknown Prime Minister by the side of the Unknown Soldier.' He was implying that Bonar Law was a mediocrity, who would not have achieved much even if he had had more time.

Lord Curzon, also present at the funeral, added that 'in days to come people would ask who he was and how he ever got there'. If Asquith's verdict was cruel, Curzon's looks like the worst kind of sour grapes: he had been passed over when Bonar Law was appointed to the premiership, though he himself and many others thought he was the best-qualified candidate for the top job.

One way or another, Asquith's waspish comment has become a kind of unofficial epitaph for Andrew Bonar Law: at least one biography of him is entitled *The Unknown Prime Minister* – though that book sets out to prove that Bonar Law was not nearly as insignificant as history has come to portray him.

It is fairer to say that Bonar Law was, however briefly, a good PM. Moreover, he was all his life a loyal party politician and a man of principle. He was also modest, saying of his own

rise to power: 'If I am a great man, then a good many of the great men of history are frauds'.

...AND EVEN MORE UNKNOWN

Henry Campbell-Bannerman is perhaps still more obscure than Andrew Bonar Law. Ask anyone to name all the prime ministers of the twentieth century, and these are the two that will stump them. At the time of his death, however, 'C-B' got a rather warmer send-off from Asquith than Bonar Law would do, 15 years later. Campbell-Bannerman, said Asquith, was 'calm, patient, persistent, indomitable. He was the least cynical of mankind, but no-one had a keener eye for the humours and ironies of the political situation. He was a strenuous and uncompromising fighter, a strong party man, but he harboured no resentment. He met both good and evil fortune with the same unclouded brow, the same unruffled temper, the same unshakeable confidence in the justice and righteousness of his cause'.

A Kingly Likeness
Prime ministers and the
royal blood

Lord North bore an uncanny similarity to the reigning monarch, George III. This strange coincidence was much commented upon during his time as prime minister. 'There appeared in the cast and formation of his countenance, nay even in his manner, so strong a resemblance to the royal family that it was difficult not to perceive it. His face might be indeed esteemed a caricature of the King,' wrote one contemporary.

People recalled that Lord North's mother, the Countess of Guilford, had been a close friend of Frederick, Prince of Wales, who was the father of the king. This fact led to speculation that there might be a scandalous explanation for the likeness between the monarch and his prime minister: surely it was possible that they were half-brothers?

Most modern historians think not: Frederick and the countess had no adulterous affair, and the physical resemblance of their respective sons is nothing more than a historical oddity.

That is not to say that no British prime minister has ever had royal blood in his veins. The family tree of David Cameron shows that he is descended from an illegitimate daughter of King William IV and his Irish mistress, Dorothea Jordan.

That daughter – one of at least ten children that Dorothea bore the king – was called Elizabeth FitzClarence. (The prefix 'Fitz-' denoted an illegitimate child of the monarch, and the king had been Duke of Clarence before coming to the throne). Elizabeth's illegitimacy was no social barrier. Her status was perfectly respectable, and everyone knew very well she was the king's daughter – in other words, a

George III

princess in all but name.

Elizabeth had no aristocratic title of her own, but in 1820, at the age of 19, she married the 18th Earl of Errol. So it was that she became the Countess of Errol, a name more fitting to her regal bloodline.

It follows that David Cameron, through his genealogical descent from the Countess of Errol and her royal father, is the fifth cousin, twice removed, of Queen Elizabeth II. But he does not look like her at all.

OLD SCHOOL TIES

Boris Johnson is the twentieth British prime minister to have been educated at Eton College. But in the past 170 years, only four premiers have been schooled at Eton's great rival, Harrow. Those four PMs were Peel, Palmerston, Baldwin and Churchill.

Three of the old Harrovian PMs – Peel, Baldwin and Churchill – had sons. And they all sent them to be educated at… Eton.

No Higher than a Policeman
Prime ministers' descriptions of the job

Being prime minister is not easy, and not everyone has been happy with the work. Some PMs have positively hated having to lead the country, others have been more or less philosophical about it. A few can be said to have enjoyed it. These are the views of some PMs on the toughest job in British politics:

I am, for the moment, *l'inévitable.'*
Lord Palmerston

' There are three classes that need sanctuary more than others: birds, wild flowers, …and prime ministers.
    Stanley Baldwin
                    ★

'I think sometimes the prime minister should be intimidating. There's not much point in being a weak floppy thing in the chair, is there?'

Margaret Thatcher

★

'Interesting work. Fine town house. Nice place in the country. Servants. Plenty of foreign travel. I wouldn't give it up if I were you.'

Harold Macmillan

★

'The main essentials of a successful prime minister are sleep and a sense of history.'

HH Asquith

★

'I feel more and more convinced of my unfitness for a pursuit which I detest, which interferes with all my private comfort, and which I only sigh for an opportunity of abandoning decidedly and for ever. Do not think that this is the language of momentary low spirits. It really is the settled conviction of my mind.'

Earl Grey

★

'I rank myself no higher in the scheme of things than a policeman – whose utility would disappear if there were no criminals.'

WE Gladstone

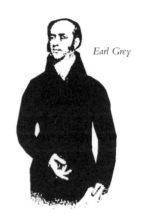

Earl Grey

★

'To have your own way, and to be for five years the Minister of this country in the House of Commons, is quite enough for any man's strength. But to be at the same time the tool of a party [the Tories] – that is to say, to adopt the opinions of men who spend their time in eating and drinking and hunting, shooting and gambling, horse-racing and so forth – this would be an odious servitude to which I would never submit.'

Robert Peel

★

'If God were to come to me and say "Ramsay, would you rather be a country gentleman than a prime minister?" I should reply: "Please God, a country gentleman.'"

Ramsay MacDonald

Beamish Boy
The unequalled brilliance of William Pitt the Younger

William Pitt the Younger was quite extraordinarily gifted. His father, who became prime minister when William was six years old, saw his son's talent, and trained him for politics from a very young age.

The young Pitt went up to Cambridge at the age of fourteen – a no less remarkable feat then than it would be now. He studied very hard, so much so that he made himself dangerously ill, and he devoted most of his efforts to rhetoric, the art of making speeches.

The teenage Pitt knew that he was destined to run the government and lead the

William Pitt the Younger

country. He became a member of parliament in 1759, at the age of 21; eighteen months later he was chancellor of the exchequer, and another eighteen months after that he was prime minister. He was then 24 years and 205 days old (almost nine years younger than the next youngest prime minister, Lord Grafton). He remained in the post (with a break of three years from 1801 to 1804) until his death at the age of 46. The Elder Pitt did not live to see anything of his precocious son's brilliant political career: he died when William was eighteen years old.

Unseated
Life after leadership

It is theoretically possible for a prime minister to lose his or her seat at a general election. This has never happened, because the party always makes certain that the PM has one of the safest seats in the country – and also because prime ministers tend to be personally popular in their own constituencies, even when the fickle electorate is turning against the party that they represent.

As a rule, modern prime ministers resign the leadership of the party if they lose a general election. James Callaghan handed over to Michael Foot after losing to Margaret Thatcher in 1979; John Major stepped down in 1997 after he was defeated by Tony Blair. (The Conservative Party then had a succession of leaders – William Hague, Iain Duncan Smith and Michael Howard – before settling on the electable David Cameron). In 2010, Gordon Brown bowed out of Downing Street once it became clear that the Tories and the Liberal Democrats were going to form a coalition against Labour.

It is now a firm tradition in British political life that ex-PMs must sit down to write their memoirs. No prime minister since Churchill has written anything that could be termed a great book, but the thick volumes of prime-ministerial reminiscences are always a political event in themselves, because they are a primary historical source, which

makes them objects of great interest to constitutionalists and political journalists.

Sometimes a prime minister's account of his years in office can breathe life into some long-dead controversy, cast light on a Westminster mystery, or just add a human dimension that was absent from the public version of events at the time. An extreme and all too memorable example of the 'human angle' is Tony Blair's toe-crimping account of how the Labour leadership contest in 1994 had a tumefacient effect on his sexual appetite.

Some ex-PMs continue to do public work while beavering away at their autobiographies. Gordon Brown remained in the House of Commons as a back-bench MP after losing the 2010 election, and seemed glad only to have one small corner of the country to worry about.

Defeated prime ministers usually have the option of accepting a peerage and continuing their careers in the House of Lords (Margaret Thatcher, for example, became Baroness Thatcher of Kesteven). Some seek a role in international politics. Tony

Blair gave up his seat in parliament and became a UN peace envoy to the Middle East, and in 2009 there were indications that he was interested in the new post of President of the European Council. In the event, he was beaten to the post by a fellow former prime minister, the little-known Belgian ex-premier, Herman von Rumpoy.

There are lots of ways for prime ministers to fill their days on leaving power. John Major went to a cricket match the day after his defeat, then went home and dug a fish pond in his garden. It is probably a fair generalisation to say that all British prime ministers find life more congenial, more enjoyable and more profitable – better in almost every way, in fact – once they stop doing the job that they fought so hard to win. 'The deed is done and I am once again a free man,' wrote Lord Grenville to his brother on leaving office. 'To you I may express what would seem to be affectation to say to others: the infinite pleasure I derive from my emancipation.'

Last Resting Place
The funerals of prime ministers

There have been some memorable prime-ministerial funerals. At the Duke of Wellington's, the man's riderless horse had pride of place behind the carriage carrying his coffin – and a pair of his trademark boots were placed backwards in the horse's stirrups. Queen Victoria attended, and remarked that 'I cannot imagine a world without him'.

Wellington was buried in St Paul's Cathedral, which is an unusual choice. The Pitts, father and son, are buried close to each other in Westminster Abbey, where several other prime ministers are to be found there, including Gladstone, Canning and Attlee. Gladstone (who was Victoria's least favourite prime minister) was transported to the cathedral, in his coffin, on the London Underground. That subterranean honour has been accorded to only one other person – not a prime minister, but the philanthropist Thomas Barnardo.

Wellington, Gladstone and Palmerston were the only three prime ministers to be given state funerals in the nineteenth century. Winston Churchill's was the only state funeral for a politician in the twentieth. It compared in terms of grandeur with Wellington's, and included an RAF flypast and a 19-gun salute.

Harold Wilson attended that funeral as serving prime minister, but his own funeral in 1995 was a low-key affair. It took place on the island of St Mary's in the Isles of Scilly, where he lived out his retirement.

Many prime ministers have chosen to be buried away from the limelight. David Lloyd George was interred before a large crowd in the land of his fathers. He chose the spot himself: he was laid to rest on the banks of the River Dwyfor, Llanystumdwy, under a stone on which he had liked to sit and think when he was a boy. His monument, a kind of ruined chapel, was designed by the Welsh architect Clough Williams-Ellis.

Edward Heath, like Lloyd George, planned every last detail of his final goodbye. The service was held at Salisbury Cathedral, in the shadow of which he spent the last 20 years of his life. The reading was from Ecclesiastes: 'Let us now praise famous men…'

THE MAGIC LANTERN

Ramsay MacDonald was the first prime minister ever to own a television set. He acquired the astoundingly novel device during his second term of office, and the engineer who installed it was none other than its inventor John Logie Baird (like MacDonald,

Harold Wilson

a Scotsman). There were almost no programmes to be seen at the time, but MacDonald felt able to say to Logie Baird that 'you have put something in my room which will never let me forget how strange the world is, and how unknown.'

Blair Play
Acting out politics

Michael Sheen as Tony Blair

One of the things modern politicians and prime ministers have to put up with is being played by actors in docu-dramas. Tony Blair is unique in that the creative (he might say fictional) re-telling of events in which he was involved began to appear while he was still PM. In the past, political figures of historical importance were rarely portrayed in their lifetimes, let alone during their time in office.

Blair has now been played three times by the same fine actor, Michael Sheen. The pieces in which Sheen has taken on the Blair role were all by the same writer, Peter Morgan. They are *The Queen*, a television drama about the events surrounding the death of Princess Diana; *The Deal*, which concerned Blair's rivalry with his chancellor and successor Gordon Brown; and *The Special Relationship*, about Blair's friendship with the US president, George W Bush.

Blair might count himself unlucky in that Sheen makes him look rather smarmy and untrustworthy. And

Sheen is so convincing in the part that Peter Morgan has even said that a passage in Blair's own memoirs (kissing the hand of the Queen when he was first elected) is taken not from real life, but from Blair's memory of seeing Sheen play the scene on screen. Blair has denied this, but the mere fact that it sounds plausible says something about Sheen's gift for performance, and also about Blair's. Both are in the business of playing to the gallery, after all.

One might think that channelling the prime minister might provide some special insight into the job or the man. Apparently not. 'Whenever

I talk about him, I'm talking about the character, rather than the actual person, because I don't have any idea about the real person,' Sheen has said. 'I don't know Tony Blair. How much similarity it bears to the actual Tony Blair, I've no idea. And I don't care.'

'This Goat-Footed Bard…'
Maynard Keynes' assessment of Lloyd George

David Lloyd George was once characterised by the great economist John Maynard Keynes as 'this extraordinary figure of our time, this siren, this goat-footed bard, this half-human visitor to our age from the hag-ridden magic and enchanted woods of Celtic antiquity.'

It is a strange and lurid description, and it seems merely to be a hostile and rather snobbish way of saying that Lloyd George was a charismatic Welshman in position of authority over well-born Englishmen. Some of Lloyd George's political manoeuvres were morally questionable, however, and this is perhaps what Keynes had in mind when he added that

he thought Lloyd George 'void and without content … one catches in his company that flavour of final purposelessness… existence outside or away from our Saxon good and evil, mixed with cunning, remorselessness, love of power.'

ONE, NOT TEN
The Duke of Wellington did not live at 10 Downing Street when he was prime minister. His home was Aspley House at Hyde Park Corner, and it gloried in the magnificent postal address of 'No.1, London'.

William Pitt and the Credit Crunch

How one prime minister tackled an economic crisis

W hen Pitt the Younger became prime minister in 1783, he inherited a situation with which David Cameron, his distant successor, would surely sympathise. The country was at the end of a long foreign war (in Pitt's case with America). The new PM had to disassociate himself from that unpopular adventure, but he still had to find the money to pay for it. Unfortunately there was no money in the government coffers. Trade and industry were at a standstill, and the national debt amounted to an unimaginably large sum (about £24 million). The prime minister had to find ways of cutting back on expenditure, while at the same time generating taxable wealth. Anything he did was bound to make him unpopular with the nation.

First, Pitt looked to trim back on wasteful expenditure in government departments. There were hundreds of people, friends and relatives of the king or of previous ministers,

who were in receipt of sinecures. As payment for some service rendered, they were given a salaried post that entailed no work. Pitt identified these time-serving office-holders and simply waited for them to die. He abolished the post if it was more or less fictional, or if there really were some duties connected with it then he made sure that they were assigned to a paid civil servant. This was naturally a slow process, but it was effective in the long run. The gradual abolition of sinecures not only saved money directly for the government, but it helped turn the civil service into a more efficient organisation.

As for generating income, Pitt's strategy was to impose hundreds of little taxes that, taken together, brought millions into the Treasury. He famously taxed windows, for example. House owners often chose to brick up windows rather than pay a duty on them, or else houses were built with bricked-up windows in anticipation of the abolition of the tax. In the event, the window duty persisted for decades, and the blind apertures with their stone frames and sills are still to be seen on many a

Georgian house. It was sometimes the practice to paint the square panes on a bricked-up window, so that a house at least looked right from a distance, and these feeble attempts at *trompe l'oeil* became known as 'Pitt's pictures'.

The window tax was vilified at the time as a tax on 'light and air'. It was nothing of the sort; it was a straightforward property tax. As a crude rule of thumb, bigger houses had more windows, and so their owners were asked to pay more tax on their home. Pitt had nothing against windows as such, and if well-to-do

people chose to deprive themselves of daylight as a means of tax avoidance, then that was their choice.

But windows were not the half of it. Pitt decided that maidservants and manservants were a taxable benefit, and he also taxed unmarried men. He placed an excise tax – an early form of VAT – on all sorts of luxuries such as clocks, hats, perfume, horses and hunting dogs. He even managed to tax wine – a brave political move that had almost destroyed previous prime ministers. It all added up to a penny-pinching, many-a-mickle fiscal policy. But it worked. Over the course of his premiership, Pitt managed to make huge inroads into the national debt, and bring about the kind of economic recovery that Cameron, at the start of his premiership, could only dream of.

Twelve Actors who have Played Churchill
Portrayals on television and in the cinema

Churchill has been portrayed hundreds of times, and some surprising people have been cast in the role. Perhaps the two most unlikely Churchills in cinematic history are John Cleese (*Decisions, Decisions,* 1975,) and Christian Slater (*Churchill: The Hollywood Years,* 2004). Here are some others on-screen Churchills:

Bob Hoskins
When Lions Roared (1994)
Joss Ackland
Above and Beyond (2006)
Mel Smith
Allegiance (2005)
Albert Finney
The Gathering Storm (2002)
Richard Burton
The Gathering Storm (1974)
Timothy West
Churchill and the Generals (1981)
Simon Ward
Young Winston (1972)
Rod Taylor
Inglourious Basterds (2009)
Robert Hardy
War and Remembrance (1989)
Howard Lang
The Winds of War (1983)
Gary Oldman
Dark Hour (2017)
Brian Cox
Churchill (2017)

Clever Clogs
The immense brains of Gladstone and Disraeli

The rivalry between Disraeli and Gladstone dominated British politics for decades. Their antagonism was interesting because, while highly gifted, they were temperamentally as different as two men could be. Many an apocryphal story contrasted Disraeli's sinuous charm with Gladstone's rather straitlaced *froideur.* There is, for example, an anecdote of a young lady who was seated next to Gladstone at dinner one evening, and next to Disraeli the following night. When she was asked to compare the two politicians she replied: 'When I left the dining room after sitting next to Mr Gladstone, I thought he was the cleverest man in England. But after sitting next to Mr Disraeli, I thought I was the cleverest woman in England.'

Bullingdon Boy
*David Cameron's time
with Oxford's posh elite*

The Bullingdon is an exclusive dining club for rich and well-connected students at Oxford University. It is a long-standing institution, dating back to 1780, and down the years members have included such well-known individuals as Otto von Bismarck, Cecil Rhodes, David Dimbleby, Edward VIII and Earl Spencer (the brother of Diana, Princess of Wales).

More than one prime minister has been a member – Lord Rosebery, for example – but David Cameron is the first premier for whom membership of the Bullingdon has been a matter of political interest.

The Bullingdon Club was virtually unknown to the broader British public until David Cameron became leader of the Conservative party in 2005. It was already common knowledge, of course, that he had been educated at Eton College, and his perceived poshness was a live political issue. How, it was asked, could a man who had enjoyed

wealth and privilege all his life lead or understand the mass of ordinary British people? What could he have in common with the millions who struggle to pay the bills, and who worry about the kind of schooling their children receive in the state system?

Part of the Conservative Party's response to this criticism was to play down Cameron's upper-middle class background. On television he was often seen in shirt-sleeves, as if a suit jacket were just a bit too stuffy for him. He set up a webcam in his home, and was shown at the kitchen sink with his hands plunged deep into the washing-up. The implied message behind the pictures was that he was well-bred, yes, and perhaps comfortably off – but essentially his life was the same as yours and mine.

This carefully cultivated image was somewhat undermined by a photograph of Cameron in his student days, posing on the steps of some Oxford college with other members of the Bullingdon Club. All of the young men in the picture are looking rather smug, not to say downright snooty. There, on the steps with Cameron, is his schoolmate Boris Johnson – later to be Prime Minister. The lean, teenage Johnson scowls at the camera from beneath that familiar long fringe of white-blond hair.

The snapshot was taken on the night of the Bullingdon Club's annual dinner, when members are obliged to wear tailcoats in navy blue with a velvet collar, ivory silk lapels, brass buttons and a mustard-coloured waistcoat. This uniform is supplied by tailors Ede and Ravenscroft at a present-day cost of about £3000, a fact that on its own speaks of a level of wealth most British voters cannot wonder at. Wedding dresses apart, how many floating voters have ever spent £3000 on a suit of clothes for a single occasion? And how many university students have that kind of money to spare?

Tory spin-doctors did their best to discourage publication of the photo – not just because of what the image said about Cameron's unusually privileged background, but also because of the rather colourful reputation of the club itself. Dinners like the one that Cameron attended

often ended in drunken rampages and acts of vandalism. There is no question that Cameron himself ever smashed up a restaurant, but the Club has on several occasions been suspended by the Oxford University authorities after a rowdy night out. As recently as 2004, four member of the Bullingdon were arrested after an Oxfordshire pub was trashed in the aftermath of a social occasion.

None of which is Cameron's fault, of course. But that photograph associates him with a kind of behaviour and lifestyle that many British people instinctively dislike. It is no surprise that the Labour Party (allegedly) considered using the picture on posters in the 2010 election campaign. The fact is that the Bullingdon snapshot is a dangerous political liability. David Cameron must surely wish that no-one had thought to take a camera along to that special night out with the boys in 1986.

One of Bellamy's Veal Pies
Last words of the prime ministers

Prime ministers are likely to be the kind of people who might give some thought to their last words, since their parting thought is bound to become part of their myth. The fact is that some said something pithy, and some didn't. Many left no known last words. Churchill, after a lifetime of phrase-making, had nothing to say at the last.

Other prime ministers died with matters of state very much on their mind. George Canning said, obscurely, 'Spain and Portugal' – presumably the answer to some question of foreign policy that troubled him as the lights dimmed in the corridors of his mind. Pitt the Elder's last words were an exhortation to his son, Pitt the Younger: 'Leave your dying father, and go to the defence of your country.' When, in the fullness of time, the younger Pitt lay on his deathbed his father's plea may still have been with him. 'Oh my country,' he cried. 'How I leave my country!'

Or maybe he didn't – because Pitt the Younger's last words are hotly disputed. An alternative deathbed account says that the last words he uttered were: 'I think I could eat one of Bellamy's veal pies.' John Bellamy was deputy housekeeper of the House of Commons, and he had recently set up a kind of snack bar within the Palace of Westminster, to provide meals to members of parliament. Pitt's remark would have been a great endorsement of Bellamy's new business venture, had it not come under such sad circumstances, and so very late in the day.

The last words of Lord Palmerston are, like Pitt's, uncertain. He may have said: 'That's article 98, now go on to the next...' while apparently under the impression that he was signing a treaty. A much more pleasing (and so far less

likely) possibility is that he said: 'Die my dear doctor? Why that's the last thing I shall do.' You can only admire a man who can joke about his own impending death – and it is better to think that he died with his wit and his wits about him.

If their last words are anything to go by, many former PMs faced up to death with existential equanimity, or with the courage born of religious belief. Neville Chamberlain remarked to Lord Halifax, two days before his death: 'Approaching dissolution brings relief.' Disraeli said at the last that 'I had rather live, but I am not afraid to die.' Henry Campbell- Bannerman averred that 'This is not the end of me.' Stanley Baldwin said simply 'I am ready.' The great political visionary David Lloyd George cried out 'The sign of the cross, the sign of the cross.' And Gladstone said a single word that signifies both faith and finality: 'Amen'.

The most touching last words, perhaps, are those, that, like Pitt's hankering for a pie, have a touch of domesticity and a love of life about them. Henry Addington's last words were 'Mary Anne', the name of the

Lloyd George

daughter who was by his bedside. The Earl of Derby, on being asked how he was feeling, said that he was 'bored to utter extinction', and then proved his point by becoming utterly extinct. Lord Rosebery asked for the music of the *Eton Boating Song* to be played as he drifted away. Harold Macmillan spoke a truer word than perhaps he knew when he said: 'I think I will go to sleep now.'

Robert Cecil's Schooldays
Lord Salisbury's hellish time at Eton

Robert Cecil, Lord Salisbury, was bullied mercilessly at Eton. He was constantly kicked and beaten by older boys, and subjected to such vicious attacks in the dining hall that he often missed meals so as to avoid getting hurt. One senior boy– a lout by the name of Troughton Major – got drunk and burned Salisbury's lip with a candle. Others vandalised his room, smashing his clock and throwing his books on the fire.

Young Robert's life became so miserable that he felt compelled to break the schoolboy code and tell on his tormenters. 'I know that you do not like complaints,' he wrote rather sweetly to his father, 'and I have tried to suppress them and conceal all this, but you are the only person to whom I can safely confide these things. Really now Eton has become perfectly unsupportable. I am bullied from morning to night without ceasing. I have no time to learn my lessons. I know this is of very little interest to you, but it relieves me to tell someone.'

Robert's father looked into his unhappy son's claims, but decided that he should remain at the school. He waited more than a year after that first letter before he withdrew young Robert from Eton, by which time the boy was an emotional wreck, on the verge of a complete breakdown. Later in life, when he became an important public figure and then prime minister, he always refused invitations to speak at his old school. In fact, if he ever saw an old Etonian in the street or around parliament he would duck out of the way – so as not to have to talk to anyone who had been with him in that fine institution.

John, Paul, George, and Harold
Wilson's desperate pursuit of popularity

Harold Wilson was one of the first prime ministers to realise the importance of popular culture, and its role in shaping the way that the PM is perceived in the country. He understood, for example, that

England's win in the 1966 World Cup was a boost to the nation's mood that he could harness – not because he had anything to do with it, but merely because he happened to be prime minister at the time. It was Wilson's idea to award MBEs to the Beatles in order to curry favour with young voters. Many holders of the order sent theirs back in disgust – as, subsequently, did John Lennon.

Wilson knew that his trademark pipe was an important part of his public persona: it somehow reminded the public that he was a down-to-earth working-class fellow, exactly the sort of person who should be running the Labour Party and the country. Wilson even went so far as to appear on the *Morecambe and Wise Christmas Show* of 1978. This was the highlight of Britain's television year – an office party for the nation, it has been called – and part of the fun was seeing respected and usually serious actors or (at the extreme of gravitas) newsreaders allowing themselves to be gently mocked.

No former PM (as Wilson was by then) had ever risked his dignity in this way, and some of his advisers

deeply disapproved. Joe Haines, Wilson's press secretary said that he was 'very depressed by the news... it's like some political Archie Rice in *The Entertainer*, doing a song and dance for a few miserable pounds.' In the broadcast show, Wilson is seen visiting the flat that Eric and Ernie shared. Wilson repeatedly causes offence to Eric, who eventually goes into a back room and returns with a large banner reading 'Maggie Rules OK'. The Maggie in question – Margaret Thatcher – was prime minister by the time another Christmas special rolled round.

Cry, Baby, Cry
The politics of tearfulness

In modern-day politics it is generally held to be a good thing if a prime minister can weep at the appropriate moment. Both Gordon Brown and David Cameron cried publicly during the 2010 election campaign and – whether their respective shows of emotion were a part of their strategy or not – it was widely accepted that they had both helped their chances by showing their feelings and their human side.

But tears have not always been approved of by prime ministers, or in prime ministers. When, in 1894, Gladstone chaired the last of his 556 cabinet meetings, all the ministers sitting around the table burst into tears. Gladstone himself remained disapprovingly dry-eyed and dubbed his colleagues 'the blubbering cabinet'.

The same adjective had earlier been pinned to the name of Viscount Goderich, who was very briefly and forgettably prime minister in 1827. Throughout his term in office he was subject to irksome and distressing attacks from other members of

Viscount Goderich

parliament, and he used to go home and weep with misery every night. When he was finally dismissed by the monarch, George IV, he cried his eyes out, and the king very kindly lent the prime minister one of his own handkerchiefs.

Another royal occasion for tears came a century later, when Stanley Baldwin was faced with managing the constitutional crisis over King Edward VIII's determination to marry Wallis Simpson, a divorcee. It fell to Baldwin to tell the king that he had to abdicate, and when he had finished delivering that difficult message he said 'Well, sir, whatever happens, my missus and I wish you happiness from the depths of our souls.' The king was so moved that he began to cry, and that set the prime minister off too.

Portrait of a Lady
The moulding of Mrs Thatcher

M argaret Thatcher was arguably the first prime minister to benefit from the attentions of a professional spin doctor. Her man behind the scenes was a TV executive named Gordon Reece. In the years before she became prime minister, he studied audience reactions to her media appearances, and concluded that she came across as 'uncaring' – not because of what she said, but because of how she said it and how she looked. Her shrill voice was a particular problem. The upper register, said Reece, was 'dangerous to passing sparrows'. He hired a coach from the National Theatre who gave Thatcher humming exercises intended to lower and deepen her vocal range. She had to practise saying the words 'The socialists must learn that enough is enough' in a way that sounded emollient and commonsensical rather than strident and aggressive. Reece also made it his business to soften her clothes and her hairstyle, to give her a womanly appeal that would make her appear unthreatening to voters of both sexes.

Reece also pioneered the use of the photo-opportunity. Thatcher was pictured pottering around the kitchen, or sitting at the piano while her adoring family looked on. She went out into communities and took charge of street-sweeping machines. The writer Matthew Parris, then a

Conservative member of Wandsworth Borough Council, saw her do this. She was crying 'Women know how to get into corners men can't reach!' as she went. Parris also once walked into a room in the House of Commons to find her standing on a chair, checking the tops of the

paintings for dust. 'It's the way a woman knows whether a room's been cleaned properly,' she said to him.

Thatcher was a woman in a man's world – or rather in the fusty old gentlemen's club that was parliament. Her special political genius was to turn this circumstance to her advantage, and Reece's brilliant idea was to draw attention to it. Thatcher made out that she was running the country on sound and very British commercial lines, as if the British economy were no more or less than her father's grocery shop writ large. It was a powerful idea – and it made her the most successful peacetime prime minister of the twentieth century.

LATE FOR DINNER

Lord Palmerston was notoriously unpunctual. He nearly always arrived late for official occasions, and once made Queen Victoria wait for dinner when she was dining with him at Brocket Hall, the stately home he had inherited through his father-in-law, the prime minister Lord Melbourne. His wife, Lord Melbourne's daughter, was just as tardy as he was. It was widely said at the time that 'the Palmerstons always miss the soup.'

Pistols at Dawn
Prime-ministerial duellists

Several PMs have been involved in duels down the years. Robert Peel was challenged to a duel by the Irish nationalist Daniel O'Connell, who objected to Peel's views on education in Ireland. The duel did not take place, because O'Connell (who was known to be a crack shot) was arrested beforehand. This was not even O'Connell's first duel with a future PM. He had himself been challenged to a duel by Disraeli in connection with some grossly antisemitic remarks that he had made.

In 1798, Pitt the Younger fought a duel with a fellow MP after a parliamentary debate about the navy got overheated. Neither participant was hurt. Shelburne fought a duel in Hyde Park in 1780, and took a bullet in the groin. He received immense public sympathy, which may well have contributed to his election as prime minister two years later. In 1809 George Canning, foreign secretary at the time, fought a duel with Lord Castlereagh, who was serving in the same cabinet as minister for war. Canning had never held a gun in his life and, predictably, he came off worst: he was hit in the leg by Castlereagh's second shot.

By far the most entertaining duel involving a prime minister was Lord Wellington's contest with fellow peer, Lord Winchilsea. Again, politics were at the root of the dispute: Winchilsea had accused the prime minister of wanting to introduce 'popery into every department of state'. This was a very ill-considered remark; when Winchilsea refused to apologise for it, Wellington wrote asking that he give 'that satisfaction which a gentleman has a right to require, and which a gentleman never refuses to give'.

The duel took place in Battersea Fields on March 21, 1829. The two men's seconds tried hard to find a deserted spot; duelling was already illegal, after all, and Wellington was breaking the law by going through with it. He quickly grew impatient with his second, Sir Henry Hardinge, who had fought alongside Wellington and lost an arm at Waterloo. 'Now then Hardinge, look sharp and step out the ground. Damn it! Don't stick him up so near the ditch. If I hit him he will tumble in.' Wellington evidently intended to shoot the man in the leg to teach him a lesson, but not to kill him.

There was in fact very little chance of the Duke hitting Winchilsea: he was an absolutely terrible marksman. If Winchilsea looked nervous (which he did), then it was because he knew that when Wellington aimed at a man's thigh there was every chance that he would hit him clean between the eyes. So it was to everyone's relief, and no-one's surprise, that Wellington missed completely with his shot. Winchilsea then gladly and ostentatiously fired his pistol into the air, and agreed to publish an apology for his remarks. Wellington immediately mounted his horse, bade Winchilsea a good day, and rode home for breakfast.

By the time Wellington had finished his meal, the duel was the talk of London. On the whole, the episode did the Duke nothing but good. 'Last week the mob were roaming hooting, abusing your father,' wrote his wife, the Duchess of Wellington, to their son. 'Now they are cheering him again.'

It was left to the philosopher Jeremy Bentham to tell the prime minister where he had gone wrong, which he did in a long, extremely po-faced and rather impertinent letter. 'Ill-advised man!... Think of the confusion into which the whole fabric of government would have been thrown had you been killed,' he wrote. 'Here am I, more solicitous for the life of the leader than he himself is… I cannot afford to lose you…'

Wellington's outing ought to have been the final duel involving a British prime minister – but it was not quite. The last prime minister to receive such a challenge was the unlikely figure of Clement Attlee. In 1935, an Italian army captain named Fanelli demanded satisfaction 'in any neutral country with any weapons' for some remarks that Attlee made in

parliament about the Italian invasion of Abyssinia. Attlee retorted that he could say what he liked in a free country, and told Captain Fanelli not to be so silly.

Herbert Henry, Henry Herbert
The changing forenames of prime minister Asquith

Asquith always signed himself 'HH Asquith' – which was just as well, as it was not always clear what his first name was.

Those two Hs stand for Herbert and Henry – in that order. His family and his friends all called him Herbert until he was forty years old. But that changed after HH's first wife died, and he married again. Asquith's new wife took to calling him Henry, and Asquith himself in effect dropped his first Christian name and began to use his second. It was as if his new remarriage constituted a different life – and that this new phase had to be marked in some way. Herbert was, in effect, dead and gone; Asquith's intimates had to get used to calling him by his other H.

THE SALISBURY BLACKS

'Salisbury blacks' is the name given to the many dark horses that drew the carriages of Lord Salisbury. All were stabled at his palatial home, and all had names that echoed the initial S of Salisbury's own. Among the Salisbury blacks were Saladin, Spice, Spirit, Sambo, Samson, Sauerkraut, Scotia, Simpleton, Sir Garnet, Sirdar, Skylark, Soldier, Soudan, Squib, Striker, Strongbow, Suakin, Suffolk, Swallow, Swift, and Swindler.

A Train of One's Own
Lord Salisbury's commute

Three-times prime minister Lord Salisbury lived at Hatfield House, a vast Jacobean manor that had been

his family's ancestral home for more than 300 years. Hatfield House was (and is) full of ancient treasures. But it was also one of the country's first modern homes. Hatfield was the first private house in England to install electric lights, and it was the first to have the benefit of a telephone.

The phone was a useful gadget for Salisbury; the electricity was, frankly, a bit of a nuisance. The wires that trailed across the floors kept overheating, and Salisbury's family often found that they were called upon to grab cushions and smother small fires.

On one occasion the cable carrying the electricity supply to the house blew down in a storm. One of Salisbury's servants, knowing no better, went to pick it up from the wet grass, and in so doing earned the sad distinction of becoming the first person in the world ever to die by electrocution.

As for Lord Salisbury himself, he loved new technology – and older technology too if it could be harnessed to make his life more convenient. One of the privileges of being prime minister was that he had a private train constantly at his disposal to take him from his Hatfield house to London. At Hatfield station there was a separate waiting room – the ancestor of the airport executive lounge, you might say – reserved for his exclusive use. He would often take the train into London after lunch, and while he was at the Commons it would wait for him at King's Cross until he was ready to go back home. It amused Salisbury to see how quickly his coachman could get him from the Palace of Westminster to the station; his record time was 17 minutes.

On one occasion Lord Salisbury boarded his private carriage in London to find that there was already someone in one of the seats. Salisbury was notoriously bad at recognising people – even old friends – and he assumed that the other traveller was someone that his wife had invited to stay for the weekend. They didn't talk on the train (this was Salisbury's nap time) but once they arrived at Hatfield House, Salisbury gave the man a lift up to the house in his brougham. Now the man – who had gone along with all this without a murmur – engaged the prime

minister in a discussion about the existence of God.

Something about the stranger's manner made Salisbury realise that both of them had made a bit of a mistake. Once they reached the house he hurried off to his study, informing a footman along the way that he had 'left a madman in the hall.'

POLITICAL HAT-TRICK
James Callaghan is perhaps the most experienced and well-qualified premier of them all. He is the only prime minister ever to have held all three of the great offices of state – Home

Secretary, Foreign Secretary and Chancellor of the Exchequer – prior to becoming prime minister.'

PMs and their Pets
Four-legged creatures in Downing Street

A goodly number of prime ministers have been fond of animals. Dogs and cats are naturally the most common pets or premiers, but parrots and budgies also figure prominently. Here is a list of prime-ministerial pets:

WE Gladstone
A Pomeranian called Petz.

Edward Heath
A mongrel called Erg (the initial letters of his forenames) and a beagle called Maggie May.

Harold Wilson
A Siamese cat called Nemo, and a dog called Paddy.

Benjamin Disraeli
Two swans called Hero and Leander.

Lord Aberdeen
Tag, a dog of indeterminate breed.

David Lloyd George
A Welsh terrier called Cymro (meaning companion); a St Bernard called Riffel (the train station in Switzerland where he bought it).

Winston Churchill
A poodle called Rufus, a budgerigar called Toby, and a cat called Margate.

Lord Shelburne
A leopard and a spaniel.

Neville Chamberlain
A retriever called Crusoe.

Henry Campbell-Bannerman
A grey parrot; dozens of bulldogs.

John Major
A collection of koi carp.

Boris Johnson
A Jack Russell-cross called Dilyn.

Cycling Dave
The two-wheeler politician

In 2006, while leader of the opposition, David Cameron was often photographed cycling to work. His commitment to his bicycle suggested youthful vigour elector-friendly green credentials. But Cameron's green tinge suddenly seemed less convincing when it turned out that he was followed most mornings by an official car carrying his briefcase and work shoes.

David Cameron

CATS IN THE CORRIDORS OF POWER

The cat at Number Ten is not so much the pet of the incumbent as an employee of the Cabinet Office. Its job is to keep mice down. In the 1960s the position was occupied by a cat named Petra. The successor to Petra was Wilberforce (named after the great reformer) who served from 1973 to 1987, under four prime ministers. Then came Humphrey, named after the officious mandarin in 'Yes, Prime Minister'. Humphrey was forced out of office by the Blairs as soon as Tony came to power. A new mouser named Sybil was brought in during Gordon Brown's tenure, but she died in office before the fall of the Labour government in 2010. The following year, television viewers spotted rats scurrying along the pavement outside Number Ten. This somehow reflected badly on David Cameron's government, so a new cat – named Larry was found for the vacant post. Cameron had been opposed to the appointment, but was persuaded to make a U-turn. 'There was a group of people in Downing Street who

thought it was a jolly good idea,' said
a spokesman. 'They have won.'

Clement Attlee, the Comic Poet
The prime-ministerial letter in verse

Clement Attlee has a reputation for being something of a cold fish – but this is unfair. He had a great sense of fun, especially when it came to children.

This rather charming aspect of his personality surely harked back to his days as the young leader of a boys' club in the East End – and the burden of high office did little or nothing to suppress it. In 1951, during his last days as prime minister, Attlee received a letter from a 15-year-old schoolgirl named Ann Glossop. She wrote to the PM to complain that she was being made to resit her School Certificate – not because she had failed, but because she was too young to qualify when she passed the exam the first time. The thing that caught Attlee's eye was that Ann Glossop had written her letter entirely in verse. This is her poetic remonstrance to the premier:

Would you please explain, dear Clement,
Just why it has to be
That certificates of education
Are barred to such as me?
I've worked through thirteen papers
But my swot is all in vain,
Because at this time next year
I must do them all again.

Please have pity, Clement,
And tell the others too.
Remove the silly age limit
It wasn't there for you.

Attlee found the time to compose a poem in response – also in verse. Here is Attlee's reply to Miss Glossop:

I received with real pleasure
Your verses, my dear Ann.
Although I've not much leisure
I'll reply as best I can.

I've not the least idea why
They have this curious rule
Condemning you to sit and sigh
Another year at school.

You'll understand that my excuse
For lack of detailed knowledge
Is that school certs were not in use
When I attended college.

George Tomlinson is ill, but I
Have asked him to explain.
And when I get the reason why
I'll write to you again.

George Tomlinson was minister for education. It is not known what steps he took when, having returned from sick leave, he found this correspondence on his desk. One likes to think that, like Attlee, he saw that Ann Glossop's talent and bravado were worth rewarding, and that he made an exception in her case.

Clem, Pee-Em
Another Attleean verse

When he was enrolled as a Knight of the Garter, Attlee was again moved to verse. He wrote a self-deprecating little limerick which he addressed to his brother Tom. It went like this:

Few thought he was even a starter
There were many who thought
themselves smarter.
But he ended PM, CH and OM,
An earl and a knight of the garter.

The letters CH, by the way, stands for Companion of Honour, and OM stands for Order of Merit.

Roses are Red, Tories are Blue
The PM who loved to arrange flowers

Alec Douglas-Home, prime minister for a year, had the unusual hobby of flower-arranging. He first took it up when he fell ill with spinal tuberculosis. According to the medical wisdom of the day, he was encased in plaster and confined to bed – where he remained, flat on his back, for two years.

During this time Douglas-Home did a great deal of reading, and he also became very good indeed at putting roses and tulips prettily in a vase. This little skill remained a part of his domestic life for decades to come 'because I was best at it, and if I didn't do it nobody else would anyway.'

Flower-arranging was also a prime-ministerial safety valve for Douglas-Home, like music was for Ted Heath, or whisky and soda for Churchill. RAB Butler said of Douglas-Home: 'Whenever things became most tense he would go away on his own for half an hour and arrange a vast bowl of flowers.'

Evil Likenesses
PMs in cartoons and satires

Right from the time the office came to be, prime ministers have been subject to mockery in political cartoons. Robert Walpole was depicted in hundreds of prints, pamphlets and scandal-sheets, and every portrayal – apart from the few he commissioned himself – is less than flattering.

Some, however, are more vicious than others. Contemporary cartoons show Walpole variously as a devil being carried by two MPs through a bog (so that no mud sticks); as the recipient of a torrent of gold issuing from the mouth of a dragon called Excise Duty (implying that he was a bribe-taker); as a slack-jawed loudmouth who could produce nothing but 'plenteous streams of mud… and noise, and impudence, and lies...' (Jonathan Swift's words).

Cartoonists had much fun with Henry Pelham's Broad-Bottomed Ministry, which (sadly for satirists) came to end in 1754. The latter half of the eighteenth and the beginning of the nineteenth century were a golden age for political cartoonists. Society was far more permissive than it was to become in later years; drawings were easy to produce and distribute; and the public appetite for scurrilous images of their leaders was at a height. A cartoon of 1783, for example, shows Lord North and his ally Charles James Fox defecating simultaneously into a big pot – which is being stirred by a rather revolted little demon. In cartoons by Gillray (one of the most vicious satirists of the age) William Pitt was often drawn as a red-nosed drunk, or at least a very heavy drinker –which he was. Gillray was offered a pension if only

he would stop portraying the prime minister in this way, an arrangement which the cartoonist cheerfully accepted.

The prime ministers who lend themselves best to being ridiculed in cartoons are those that have an easily recognisable prop or quirk or personal characteristic. This feature can be almost anything: with Pitt it was his pencil-like lankiness; with Lord Russell, conversely, his extreme smallness of stature.

In Disraeli's case it was his Jewishness – or at any rate his middle-eastern appearance: in cartoons he was parodied as 'Ben JuJu', and he appeared in the guise of a Moses, a Shylock, an Egyptian sphinx or a street pedlar wearing three hats (a common Victorian stereotype of a Jew). Later prime ministers have had less sinister signifiers: in the world of cartoons, Churchill is always equipped with a cigar, Wilson with a pipe, Chamberlain with his umbrella, and Thatcher with her formidable handbag.

The most recent prime ministers have been harder for the caricaturists to pin down. Major had his strange upper lip, like a rabbit's, which came in handy for some cartoonists. Steve Bell (perhaps the greatest modern political cartoonist) made use of the story, circulated by a pro-Labour journalist, that Major habitually tucked his shirt into his underpants.

But not one of the five PMs who have followed after Major provided their mockers with an obvious visual hook: Tony Blair's preening self-confidence, Gordon Brown's dour and grumpy demeanour, David Cameron's boyish visage – none of these are instantly translate to a recognisable cipher on the printed page. Perhaps it is the case that, these days, prime ministers need to look less remarkable – to be more altogether less extraordinary – to get elected in the first place.

WRONG CALL

'It will be years before a woman either leads the Party or becomes prime minister. I don't see it happening in my time.' So said Margaret Thatcher in 1974, the year before she was elected leader of the Conservative party, and five years before becoming prime minister.

Wilson, a Russian spy?
Cloak-and-dagger stuff at Number Ten

Harold Wilson was paranoid about plots against him. He believed that the Cabinet Room was bugged, and that one of the devices was hidden in the wall behind the portrait of Gladstone. He even called in a South African security firm to check the room, but the experts concluded that there was nothing more sinister behind the canvas than the remains of an old light fitting.

But there lay a real political fear behind Wilson's suspicious view of the Gladstone painting; he felt sure that the British security services were against him, and that they were working in clandestine ways to overthrow his government. Wilson's worries later gained credence from

remarks published in *Spycatcher*, the 1987 memoir of MI5 agent Peter Wright. According to Wright, some people in MI5 believed that Wilson was a communist and a KGB agent. Wright says that he heard colleagues make remarks such as 'Wilson's a bloody menace and it's about time the public knew the truth,' and 'We'll have him out, this time we'll have him out.' Plot or not, it is certainly true that, in the climate of the cold war, the security services were less sympathetic to left-wing governments than to right-wing ones.

In more recent times, there have been serious claims that the Cabinet Room, and other rooms at Number Ten, were indeed bugged during the 1960s and 1970s. The suggestion, which has not been published, is that in the wake of the Profumo affair in 1963 listening devices were installed on the orders of then prime minister Harold Macmillan. The bugs (it is said) were removed during the incumbency of James Callaghan.

If this were true, then the bugs would have been in place throughout Wilson's regime. Perhaps he was not so paranoid after all.

A Period of Silence
The man-of-few-words style of Attlee

A ttlee served as Churchill's deputy in the wartime cabinet, and succeeded him as PM at the first election after the war. It is hard to imagine two more diametrically opposed personalities. Churchill was egotistical, voluble, sure of his own place in history. Attlee was quiet-mannered, unprepossessing, totally devoid of the charisma that surrounded Churchill like a bright shining aura.

But the absence of glamour was not necessarily a disadvantage to Attlee: it meant he was not greedy for the political limelight, and so he never made rash, self-aggrandising decisions.

Churchill is said to have remarked that Attlee was 'a modest man, but then he has much to be modest about.' If he did say that (and there is no reliable record of it), then he would have been doing no more than teasing, because he would have known that assessment was unfair.

Attlee, on the other hand, was closer to the mark when he told

Churchill, at the end of one of his long cigar-chewing declamations, that 'a monologue is not a decision'.

Attlee's ability to puncture Churchill's oratory came in useful after the 1945 election, when they were no longer on the same coalition team, but facing each other across the floor of the House. His famous terseness came almost as a relief after the relentlessly florid eloquence of his predecessor. One of Attlee's aides said that 'he would never use one syllable where none would do. And the king, who by age-old tradition had to meet with his prime minister once a week, referred to the man everyone else called Clem as 'Clam'.

Attlee's inclination to brevity was not just a political attitude; it extended to ordinary conversation. A veteran of World War I, he was once asked by the US ambassador whether he had ever done any big-game hunting. This was a rather odd question to ask a socialist MP, but Attlee answered briefly that he had. 'What did you shoot?' asked the ambassador. 'Germans,' said Attlee.

He liked others to be as parsimonious with words as he was himself. He once told Professor Harold Laski, chairman of the Labour party, that 'a period of silence on your part would be welcome'. And he said that 'democracy means government by discussion – but it is only effective if you can stop people talking.'

STONY PORTLAND

Clement Attlee was not the only, or even the most taciturn prime minister. The Duke of Portland, it was said, 'possessed in an eminent degree the talent of dead silence.' In his case it was due to an almost pathological shyness.

The Duke of Portland

Harold Macmillan

Lords, namely Lord Kilmuir and Lord Salisbury (who was the grandson of the Victorian prime minister, the 3rd Marquess of Salisbury).

The incumbent Lord Salisbury was afflicted with a slight speech impediment which meant that he could not pronounce his 'r's. So it was that he greeted each of the advancing cabinet members with the memorable question: 'Well, which is it, Wab or Hawold.'

After Anthony
Choosing the successor to Eden

When Anthony Eden resigned in the wake of the Suez crisis, the Conservative party was faced with a choice between RAB Butler and Harold Macmillan. The man that they chose would be prime minister at least until the next election.

All the newspapers expected the job to go to Butler, but the Tory leadership had its own arcane ways of selecting a leader, and it kept its own counsel. All the outgoing members of Eden's cabinet were summoned separately to a meeting with their two most senior colleagues in the house of

Allure of the Handbag
The feminine charms of Margaret Thatcher

Mrs Thatcher, at the height of her power, seems to have exerted a powerful attraction on the men who surrounded her. Alan Clark, who served under her as trade and defence secretary, confided to his diary that he found the prime minister 'very attractive – I never came across any other woman in politics as sexually attractive in terms of eyes, wrists and ankles'.

The writer Kingsley Amis said that she was 'one of the most beautiful women I have ever met,' and Dr Josef

Margaret Thatcher

a woman who possessed such force of character and such political clout.

President Mitterand of France got close to the mark when he said that Thatcher had 'the eyes of Caligula but the mouth of Marilyn Monroe.'

'Crisis? What Crisis?'
The damaging quote that never was

Luns, Secretary-General of NATO, described her straightforwardly as 'sexy'. The Tory MP Nicholas Fairbairn once saw a tipsy guest at an official reception accost Mrs T to tell her how much he fancied her. 'Quite right,' she replied. 'You have very good taste but I just do not think you would make it at the moment.'

Some of Thatcher's allure was surely no more or less than the magnetic effect of power, and one wonders if a connoisseur of lechery such as Clark would have felt the same frisson about Thatcher if she had not been his boss or – come to that – the unassailable leader of the nation. For him, as for many of her admirers, there was something beguiling about

The bitterly cold winter of 1978, the last of Jim Callaghan's premiership, was a time of strikes, shortages and industrial strife. Britain was at war with itself, and the mood was grim.

At the start of winter, bread was briefly rationed when a strike by bakers led to panic-buying. Gravediggers in Liverpool walked out, with the result that dead bodies had to kept stacked in warehouses until they could be buried. Rubbish went uncollected, and mountainous piles of trash built up on Leicester Square, which became a playground for hordes of rats. Lorry drivers, fighting for a 25 per cent pay rise, prevented the delivery of materials for making penicillin, and hospitals began to run short. Ambulance drivers, meanwhile, announced their intention to ignore 999 calls, and a leader of their union said that 'if it means lives lost, that is how it must be.' The London *Evening Standard*, right at the start of the crisis, called it the 'winter of discontent' – and the phrase stuck fast.

In the midst of all this, prime minister James Callaghan jetted off to Guadaloupe for a summit meeting with other heads of state. On his return, the press were waiting for him at the airport on his return, and against the advice of his advisers he agreed to an impromptu press conference, intending to present a calm assessment of the situation. As Callaghan stood in front of the TV cameras, a reporter asked him 'What is your general approach, in view of the mounting chaos in the country at the moment?' Callaghan said: 'That's a judgement that you are making. I promise you that if you look at it from outside, and perhaps you're taking rather a parochial view at the moment, I don't think that other people in the world would share the view that there is mounting chaos.'

That rather anodyne response,

spoken with the honest intention of reassuring the British public, was big news the next day. *The Sun* printed it under the headline 'Crisis? What Crisis?', alongside a photograph of Callaghan looking tanned and relaxed. The doubly misleading impression created by that front page was that Callaghan had been on holiday while the country was imploding, and that the phrase in the headline was the exact one that he had used. *The Sun*'s paraphrase almost immediately attained the status of a direct quotation, which did immense damage to Callaghan's personal prestige and to the government's popularity. In March the Labour government fell, having lost a motion of no confidence by a single vote. And in May, Callaghan was booted out of office – dogged and damned by words that he never uttered.

NO FIRST LADY

Only four prime ministers in history have been unmarried. They are Lord Wilmington, William Pitt the Younger, Arthur Balfour, and Edward Heath. Only three PMs have been divorced:

Duke of Grafton

the Duke of Grafton, Anthony Eden and Boris Johnson.

A Melancholy Pacifist
The unhappy life and premiership of the Earl of Aberdeen

The Earl of Aberdeen, prime minister from 1852 to 1855, was a cousin of the poet Lord Byron – and like Byron, he was given to long periods of sadness.

Unlike Byron, however, he had plenty of reasons to be unhappy. Aberdeen was orphaned as a child, and his first wife, whom he adored, died of tuberculosis at the age of 28. Her name was Catherine Hamilton, and she was a famous beauty. When she died, it was said, 'the sunshine went out of his life forever'.

Aberdeen's three daughters by that marriage all succumbed to tubercular disease in their teens. The last of them, his beloved Alice, died in his arms. After these tragedies, Aberdeen's mop of curly dark hair turned white and grew thin. Like Queen Victoria, he wore mourning black for the rest of his life.

Aberdeen was a fine classical scholar and archaeologist. In his youth he conducted important excavations in Athens. Along with Lord Elgin, he was responsible for removing many important reliefs from the Acropolis and bringing them back to Britain. For this act Elgin and Aberdeen were roundly and publicly criticised by the Grecophile Byron, family ties notwithstanding. They 'make their grand saloons a general mart,' wrote the poet, in not very good verse, 'for all the mutilated blocks of art.'

In 1802, on his way to Greece, Aberdeen had made the acquaintance of Napoleon Bonaparte. The future emperor was then First Consul, and France was uneasily at peace with

George Hamilton-Gordon, 4th Earl of Aberdeen

Britain. A decade later Aberdeen witnessed the Battle of Leipzig, also known as the 'Battle of Nations'. This encounter involved about 600,000 French and German troops. It was the largest battle ever to have taken place in Europe, and remained so until the grim set-pieces of World War I finally outdid it. The battle lasted three days, and it cost the lives of more than 100,000 men.

His bystander's experience of battle left Aberdeen with a lifelong horror of warfare. 'I consider war to be the greatest folly, if not the greatest crime, of which a country could be guilty,' he said in the Commons. 'And I agree entirely with a moral writer who has said that if a proof were wanted of the deep and thorough corruption of human nature, we should find it in

the fact that war itself was sometimes justifiable'. He did his best to live by that conviction. As foreign secretary under the Duke of Wellington and then Robert Peel, Aberdeen pursued a peace-making agenda. But it was his great political misfortune to succeed to the premiership at a time when the country was drifting towards war with imperial Russia.

In 1854, the second year of his premiership, Aberdeen felt compelled to order the British fleet into the Black Sea, so as to protect Britain's ally, Turkey. Reluctantly, he issued an ultimatum to the Russians, demanding that their fleet return to port in Sebastopol. The Russians refused, and war was declared.

The Crimean war was conducted with huge incompetence by the British commanders on the ground, and the troops that were despatched to besiege Sebastopol endured terrible hardship. The public was made well aware of the bungling of the generals and the suffering of British rank-and-file thanks to the brilliant front-line reports of William Russell, *The Times*'s correspondent on the spot. It is a bitter irony that the Earl of Aberdeen, a principled opponent of war, received all the blame for conducting this war badly. His predecessor Lord Derby went so far as to say: 'I believe this war would never have taken place if the noble earl opposite had not been the minister at the head of government'. When parliament set up a committee of enquiry into the management of the Crimean episode, Aberdeen resigned. He had been brought low by scathing journalism, low public opinion, parliamentary mistrust, and his own distaste for the policy he had to pursue.

The years that remained to the former prime minister were spent with his books and what his cousin Byron (now long dead) had called his 'misshapen monuments and maimed antiques'.

The verdict on Aberdeen's style as prime minister was pronounced by Disraeli, who in 1853 had written this unkind description:

'His manner, arrogant yet timid – his words, insolent and yet obscure – offend even his political supporters. His hesitating speech, his contracted sympathies, his sneer, as icy as Siberia, his sarcasms, drear and barren as the steppes, are all characteristic of the bureau and the chancery, and not of popular and aristocratic assemblies animated by the spirit of honour and the pride of gentlemen.'

ABERDEEN'S MARBLES

Many of the ancient artefacts that the Earl of Aberdeen acquired in Athens now form part of the antiquities collection at the British Museum. An exception is the so-called 'foot of Hercules', a marble fragment that once formed part of the huge frieze that ran around the exterior of the building, above the heads of the columns. That priceless limb had been in Athens for thousands of years until Aberdeen

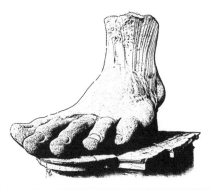

brought it to Britain, but some time afterwards it was lost. Nobody knows what has become of it.

Bute on the Back Foot
Britain's most unpopular prime minister

The Earl of Bute was a deeply disliked prime minister, and he achieved his unpopularity in a very short time – just 317 days over the course of 1762 and 1763. There were many reasons that he was unloved by the British public, and one of them was that he loved himself so dearly. He was extremely vain, and took great pride in his shapely legs, which he showed off in amateur theatricals.

Another reason for the low esteem in which he was held in England was that he was born a Scot. He was in fact the first Scottish-born prime minister of Great Britain (and also the first Tory). Bishop Warburton said of him: 'Lord Bute is a very unfit man to be a prime minister of England. First, he is a Scotchman; second, he is the King's friend; and thirdly, he is an honest man.'

The third charge against Bute makes the bishop's remark look like an ironic dig at Bute's detractors. But the second charge – that he was the 'King's friend' – seems to be voicing a genuine and widespread suspicion that Bute exercised undue influence over George III. It was also said that he was on rather too friendly terms with Augusta, the Dowager Princess of Wales, who was the young king's mother. This scurrilous accusation was often graphically and obscenely alluded to in political squibs and cartoons.

None of this sniping did his popular standing much good, but perhaps the chief reason for his unpopularity was his decision to put a tax on cider. There was an outcry among the drinking classes, and something akin to an uprising in the cider-producing areas of the country. On one occasion he was

Earl of Bute

attacked by an angry mob on his way to a banquet in Guildhall.

Though his time in office was brief, Bute's legacy is longer-lasting and diverse. By way of example, he arranged an annual pension of £300 a year for the lexicographer Samuel Johnson, which meant that the great man of letters could live and work without fear of poverty. The Dictionary might never have come to fruition but for Bute.

Bute seems to have been a gifted talent-spotter. He appointed the architect Robert Adam as Surveyor of the King's Works (Adam had remodelled Bute's own house at Luton Hoo). This decision led to the construction of some fine buildings in London.

Thirdly, and just as laudably, Bute's keen interest in plants led him to encourage and help Princess Augusta in her attempt to establish the garden at Kew – which remains one of the great repositories of botanical specimens in the world, as well as one of Britain's best and most worthwhile tourist attractions. A species of tree, *Butea superba*, is named after the largely forgotten Earl of Bute.

ALL CHANGE
The year 1834 is unique in that it saw four prime ministers: Earl Grey (up until July 9th), Lord Melbourne (16th July to November 14th), the Duke of Wellington (November 17th to December 9th), and Robert Peel (December 10th through to April the following year).

Four Things Named after Prime Ministers
Eponymous prime-ministerial paraphernalia

Here are some things that bear the names of British prime ministers: a kind of bag, a kind of bowl, a kind of hat, and a bunch of Albanian boys.

The Gladstone bag
A Gladstone bag is a copious soft-leather case with a hinged opening at the top – like a giant but still rather chic clasp handbag. The original was produced by a leather-shop owner named JG Beard, whose premises were in Westminster, close

to parliament. He based the design on a type of bag already well-known in France, and named his version after the prime minister, whom he greatly admired. The bag quickly became established as an early design classic. Wilde gives it a mention in his story *The Picture of Dorian Gray*: 'What a way for a fashionable painter to travel. A Gladstone bag and an Ulster.' (An Ulster is a kind of overcoat.)

The writer Joseph Conrad always travelled with a Gladstone bag – and so do many of his adventurous characters. Gladstone bags were a standard piece of kit for doctors making house visits throughout the first half of the twentieth century.

Rockingham ware

Rockingham ware is a kind of porcelain made on estate of the Earl of Rockingham, at Swinton in Yorkshire. The style of Rockingham ware is florid and ornate, like a nineteenth-century version of rococo. An entire Rockingham dessert service was presented to William IV during his reign. It passed to Queen Victoria after his death, and can still be seen at Windsor Castle.

But the most famous piece of Rockingham is the Rhinoceros Vase. This huge piece was, at the time it was made, the largest porcelain object to have been fired in one piece anywhere in the world. It was created in 1826 to demonstrate the skill of the Rockingham potters, and is an astonishing object: 1.2 metres high, 50kg in weight, and fabulously decorative. The body of the vase is painted with a still life of wilting flowers; the handles are two complex garlands of gilded oak leaves, and the lid sports a stylised golden rhinoceros.

The Anthony Eden

The Anthony Eden was a style of hat favoured by Eden in the 1930s, when he was foreign secretary. The hat was in effect a stiff homburg with a single neat dent running down the centre of the crown. The hat became Eden's trademark. He was presented with one in the Lancashire hat-making town of Atherton as late as 1955, while campaigning for election. By this time, hats of all sorts were rapidly going out of fashion in Britain.

Nine Kosovan Tony Blairs

In 1999, during the Yugoslav wars, Tony Blair supported the use of NATO air attacks on Serbian targets in Kosovo. The aim of the action was to force the attacking Serbs to withdraw, and so help the Albanian population of the region. The NATO strikes were highly controversial, but largely successful. The Kosovo Albanians were thankful to NATO, and to Tony Blair in particular, for intervening on their behalf.

As a strange consequence of the Kosovan people's gratitude, a number of Albanian boys born in 1999 were given the forename 'Tonibler' – an Albanian conflation of the prime minister's full name. In 2010, after leaving office, Blair went to Kosovan capital of Pristina and met nine of his 10-year-old namesakes. One of them, Tonibler Sahiti, ventured the opinion that Tony Blair was 'a very great man'.

And the proud mother of one of the Toniblers said; 'I hope to God that he grows up to be like Tony Blair, or just a fraction like him.'

PRIME MINISTERS AND THE ZODIAC

More prime ministers have been born under Libra, the sign of the scales, than under any other star sign. There have been eight Libran PMs in all, among them both Thatcher and May. Pisces and Aries are the next most common birth sign among prime ministers, with six each. Only two prime ministers have been Sagittarians – but they were both memorable ones: Disraeli and Churchill. More prime ministers have been born on a Wednesday, and more have died on a Tuesday, than on any other day of the week.

The Iron Teddybear
The Duke of Wellington's soft spot for children

The Duke of Wellington could be a terrifying person to encounter, but he was soft as butter when it came to children.

On one occasion he encountered a small boy sobbing in the street. He stopped to ask the lad what was wrong, why he was upset. The boy said that he was due to be sent away to school the next day, and that once he was gone there would be nobody to look after his pet toad.

The Duke immediately promised to look after the toad himself. A week later he sent a letter to the boy at his new school. 'Field Marshall the Duke of Wellington presents his compliments to Master ——,' it read, 'And has the pleasure to inform him that his toad is well.'

Four More Things Named after PMs
A tea, a town, a faithful promise and an item of footwear

Here are some more eponyms – just to show that history sometimes remembers British prime ministers for things other than their prime-ministering.

Earl Grey tea
The legend of Earl Grey tea states that a Chinese mandarin gave the recipe for bergamot-infused tea to Lord Grey after one of his men saved the mandarin's son from drowning.

It is difficult to see when this incident might have happened, since Earl Grey never set foot in China. A more plausible version is that a box of the tea was presented to him as a diplomatic gift – either when he was foreign minister under Grenville, or when he was prime minister.

However it came about, it is a fact that Earl Grey got hold of some tea that came to be known by his name. The tea proved so popular with visitors to Grey's home that he passed the recipe on to a tea merchant

– some say Jackson's, others Twining's – who were charged with producing it commercially. The version of the story told at the Earl Grey Tea House in Howick (ancestral home of the Grey family) is that a Chinese mandarin was indeed involved, and that the citrussy tea was specially formulated to counter the limey waters of the Howick estate. One certain fact about Earl Grey tea is that the family never registered it as a trademark, and so have never made any money from the use of the name of the distinguished second earl.

The Balfour Declaration

The Balfour Declaration is a promise that Arthur Balfour, then foreign secretary, made in 1917 in a letter to Baron Rothschild, the leader of Britain's Jewish community.

The letter stated that: 'His Majesty's government view with favour the establishment in Palestine of a national home for the Jewish people, and will use their best endeavours to facilitate the achievement of this object, it being clearly understood that nothing shall be done which may prejudice the civil and religious rights of existing non-Jewish communities in Palestine, or the rights and political status enjoyed by Jews in any other country.'

The letter paved the way for the Jewish state of Israel. There are streets named after Balfour in both Tel Aviv and Jerusalem.

Pittsburgh, Pennsylvania

Fort Pitt, later the city of Pittsburgh, Pennsylvania, is named after William Pitt the Elder. The name was coined by the English general John Forbes, who wrote to Pitt in 1758 saying: '... I have used the freedom of giving your name to Fort Du Quesne, as I hope it was in some measure the being actuated by your spirits that now makes us Masters of the place...'

In 1890 the United States Board on Geographic Names decreed that all US place names ending in –burgh should be standardised to –burg, without the final 'h'. For twenty years, Pittsburgh was known as Pittsburg, until an exception was made in Pittsburgh's case because of its long and venerable history.

The Wellington boot

The original wellington was not the

rubber gumboot that we know today. It was a leather military boot, not unlike a jackboot.

The connection with the Duke of Wellington is real. After Waterloo, the Duke asked his bootmaker, Hoby of St James's, to make a boot for him that was less fussy than the tassled 'Hessian boot' then worn by British officers. Hoby produced a high boot with rounded toes and no decorative stitching, something designed to be worn underneath the trousers.

The unadorned boot was swiftly adopted by Beau Brummel, the Regency dandy. He was a good friend of Wellington's, and he took to wearing the boots outside his tight-fitting pantaloons. Brummel's seal of approval made wellies (as they began to be called even then) an essential item of footwear for a fashionable Englishman. To be considered proper wellingtons, however, they had to be handmade at Hoby's.

The exclusivity of wellingtons evaporated in the 1850s, when manufacturers began to make them from rubber, a new material that was beginning to be imported from plantations in South America. The process of vulcanisation, whereby raw rubber was rendered hard but malleable, had recently been discovered by Charles Goodyear.

Simultaneous advances in the mechanisation of shoe-making meant that it was now possible to turn out comfortable, waterproof boots in industrial quantities. Wellies were democratised as a direct result of these technological leaps, and became standard issue for common soldiers in armies around the world.

In the twentieth century, and up to the present, they have been an integral part of the civilian attire of farmers, festival-goers, firemen, and puddle-jumping five-year-olds.

The Earl of Shelburne

in life he amassed a large collection of books, and employed the philosopher and scientist Joseph Priestley as his personal librarian.

SELF-MADE MAN OF LETTERS

The Earl of Shelburne, for all that he was a high-born aristocrat, was perhaps the worst-educated prime minister ever to have taken office. He was born and brought up in Ireland. 'From the time I was four years old till I was fourteen,' he said, 'my education was neglected to the greatest degree.' Of his later studies he wrote: 'I was sent first to an ordinary publick school, I was then shut up with a tutor.' At the age of eighteen he went to Oxford, but left university without taking a degree. He then joined the 20th Regiment of Foot as a junior officer, and the army became his university of life. He turned out to be a spectacularly good soldier, and left the army after three years with the rank of colonel. Later

Trouble with Gladstone
The most insufferable prime minister of them all

In many ways William Ewart Gladstone cut an unattractive figure. He was, for example, an inveterate penny-pincher. His entire adult life he kept a daily account of every ha'penny he spent. This fiscal ledger extends over 65 years, and it runs to 41 volumes. It is a tedious monument to single-minded prudence.

Gladstone's personal parsimony became a kind of political virtue during the time that he served as chancellor of the exchequer. One of his first acts in that role was to insist that Foreign Office officials use smaller, cheaper sheets of paper for their endless memoranda. He justified this kind of economy by saying that 'no chancellor is worth his salt who is not ready to save by candle-ends and cheese-parings in the cause of his country.'

William Gladstone

But far more off-putting than Gladstone's stinginess was his insufferable self-importance. Queen Victoria was mortified when Gladstone was elected for a second time, and said that she 'will sooner abdicate than have anything to do with that half-mad firebrand, who would soon ruin everything and be a dictator'. She had to put up with him, of course, but continued to complain that 'he speaks to me as if I were a public meeting'.

Destruction of a Masterpiece
The lost last portrait of Winston Churchill

In 1954, on the occasion of his 80th birthday, Winston Churchill attended a celebration at the House of Commons in which he was presented with a portrait of himself. The painting had been commissioned by all the members of parliament collectively, and it was the work of the distinguished war artist Graham Sutherland. Churchill had sat for the portrait at his home in Chartwell, but had never seen the finished work before the presentation ceremony. When the picture was unveiled, Churchill showed every sign of being delighted. 'It is a remarkable example of modern art,' he said graciously – and ever so slightly ambiguously.

Because he hated it. His immediate dislike of the portrait was partly due to the fact that he had expected to be shown in the lordly regalia of a Knight of the Garter – since that was what he had worn when sitting for Sutherland – but in the finished work he was shown in Commons' garb, an ordinary suit. The MPs who had commissioned the picture had insisted upon this change; the portrait was a gift from parliament to its greatest parliamentarian, after all. But for Churchill, to be stripped of his robes felt like a kind of demotion.

More materially, Churchill loathed the depiction of his face. He had suffered a stroke some years before, and his features tended to droop if he stayed still and silent for long. Sutherland had compensated for this by making use of photographs of Churchill when painting the face. But nevertheless the man in the picture looked aged, frail, and perhaps a little confused. Lady Clementine, Churchill's wife, later said that the portrait depicted 'a gross monster'. Churchill himself was just as blunt: 'It makes me look like an idiot,' he is said to have remarked, 'Which I ain't.'

Churchill took the portrait home – and it was never seen again. Some say that it was smashed up and fed into the wood-burning boiler at his London residence. Others maintain that it went to Chartwell, where it was thrown on a bonfire like a kind of two-dimensional Guy Fawkes puppet. However it came about, there is no doubt that the painting was secretly disposed of quite soon after it was presented.

The fate of the picture became known after Churchill's death in 1965. Sutherland said that the destruction of his work was an act of vandalism. Others pointed out that whatever Churchill may have thought of it personally, the Sutherland portrait was a valuable and significant work of art and should not have been burned on the sitter's whim. For admirers of Sutherland's oeuvre, there was some consolation in the fact that his many sketches and trial runs have survived (and some of these can still be seen in the National Portrait Gallery in London).

But in the end it was Churchill's opinion of the painting that mattered. He was, among many other things, a fine historian, and he cared how he would be remembered by history. He did not want to be wheeled out in front of later generations as a decrepit old man, so he decided unilaterally that posterity could do without Sutherland's vision of him. He may have been wrong in his judgment, but he surely had the right to make it.

'Give it to Brown…'
Salisbury's inability to put a name to a face

L ord Salisbury was terrible at remembering people – a problem that was exacerbated by his poor eyesight. Once he was walking through Westminster with his private secretary, and was greeted warmly by a gentleman coming the other way. 'Who was that man?' Salisbury asked his secretary – who told him that the man was a government minister who had been in Salisbury's cabinet for the past two years.

Another story, possibly apocryphal, relates how Salisbury was given a list of possible candidates for ambassador to some small and distant country. He looked through the list, not recognising any of the names – but the last one on the list caught his eye. 'Brown, Brown,' he said. 'That's a good English name. Give it to Brown.'

Hamish and the Sorceress
Ramsay MacDonald's love for Lady Londonderry

T he pressures of being prime minister are huge, and many of the men who have held the job have found support and solace in the company of a woman. Sometimes that woman was the prime minister's wife, sometimes not.

The most remarkable such romance was between Ramsay MacDonald, lowborn leader of Britain's first Labour government, and the haughty Edith Castlereagh, Marchioness of Londonderry. They met for the first time in 1924, and the occasion was a dinner at Buckingham Palace. The newly elected socialist premier, who was the illegitimate son of Lossiemouth seamstress, found himself seated next to the Marchioness, who was known to be opposed to everything that socialism stood for.

Despite the social and political gulf between them, MacDonald and Lady Londonderry hit it off immediately. Both had a love for the Scottish highlands, and for the colourful tales of Celtic mythology, and this smoothed conversation at first. On a more emotional level, both were profoundly lonely. MacDonald's wife had died thirteen years before, and he never found another companion. (When he was asked why he had not remarried, he replied 'I buried my heart in 1911'.) Lady Londonderry, for her part, was married to a man who was a habitual adulterer. She was only occasionally the centre of her husband's affections.

MacDonald and Lady Londonderry began to correspond soon after their first meeting. She and her husband were the first people he invited to come and stay at Chequers, the prime minister's grace-and-favour country house. She soon became a close friend, his sounding board and his solace. In the midst of dull meetings with trade-unionists he would scribble *billets doux*, which would be despatched to her at her palatial home, Londonderry House. At the end of a long day, he would sometimes go and have supper with her, and offload the cares of the day. 'The burden of Atlas was nothing to mine,' he said to her. 'His was the world; mine is the follies of the world.'

As time went on, they became closer. 'No one is with me here today,' MacDonald wrote from Chequers. 'By the fire in the long gallery I sit alone. The Cromwell portraits look down through the shadowy light and are the only company I have…' In a yet more melancholy moment, he wrote: 'The day is sure to come when I shall again be of the sea and the mist, and you will continue to reign at your fireside and amongst your own people. "I once knew him," you will say, and maybe sigh. And that will be all.'

In 1931, during MacDonald's troubled second term, she wrote: 'My dearest H, I feel so worried about you. What is it? Shall I come and see you

Ramsay MacDonald

tomorrow morning – or what would you like me to do? You wrote me such a very charming and dear letter; I cannot bear to think of you worried and wretched. This letter carries all my love to you and the flowers. Bless you, and more love from C.'

The initial 'H' with which Edith addressed MacDonald stood for Hamish. This was the pet appellation he had been given when he became a member of her Ark, a kind of secret little club that met at her house on Wednesdays. Every member was given both a name and an animal or mythological being that became their Ark persona: MacDonald was Hamish the Hart; she was Circe the Sorceress – hence the monogrammatic 'C' with which she signed her letters to the prime minister.

The tone of those letters suggests otherwise, but MacDonald and Lady Edith were never lovers. They were intimate in every other sense, though. And inevitably, their deep affection for each other spawned all kinds of rumours in Westminster and beyond.

In Labour circles, disapproval of MacDonald's dalliance had less to do with any perceived impropriety as with the class betrayal that the friendship implied.

'Why the castles of the wealthiest, most aristocratic, most reactionary of the Conservative Party?' wrote Beatrice Webb. 'Because, JRM would answer if he laid bare his heart, I am more at home with them than with you or any other member of the Labour Party.... He ought not to be more at home in the castles of the great than in the homes of his followers. It argues a perverted taste and a vanishing faith.'

Fears about MacDonald's class allegiance seemed justified when, in 1930, he agreed to lead a national government in collaboration with the Tories. His Labour comrades were stunned, and for this betrayal he was expelled from the party. The long years of hard work had in any case destroyed his health. He resigned the premiership in 1935, and died suddenly in 1937. As for Lady Londonderry, she continued to love and support him, even after he was dead. He 'loved beautiful things,' she wrote in her memoirs. 'Books, pictures, beautiful women, and lovely jewels and colours. And why shouldn't he? He was, for these days, and old-fashioned socialist. His aim was to improve, not to destroy.'

ALL ABOARD THE ARK

Ramsay Macdonald was not the only prime minister – past or future – to be a member of Lady Londonderry's exclusive Ark.

Winston Churchill was a Wednesday regular, and he went under the name of Winston the Warlock. Balfour was often there too, and he was known Arthur the Albatross. Harold Macmillan's appellation was Harold the Hummingbird, Stanley Baldwin was 'the Bear', and Chamberlain was 'Neville the Devil'.

Other distinguished members of the Ark included Cabinet Secretary Maurice Hankey (Cyril the Squirrel), as well as the writers James Barrie and John Buchan ('the Bard' and 'the Buck', respectively). Nancy Astor was 'the Gnat'); Sir Samuel Hoare, 'Sam the Skate'). Most highly placed of all was Prince Albert – the future George VI – who was known in deferentially, in reference to the royal coat of arms, as 'the Unicorn'.

A Home for Alec
A man between two houses

Alec Douglas-Home was the last blue-blooded aristocrat to lead the country as prime minister. On the death of his father, 13th Earl of Home, he went from the Commons to the House of Lords. Then, uniquely in the British political history, he disclaimed his peerage so that he could return to the Commons and take the job of PM.

The fact that Douglas-Home had deliberately shinned a few rungs down the social ladder in order to serve did not stop opposition leader Harold Wilson indulging in a little inverted snobbery. 'After half a century of democratic advance,' said Wilson, 'the whole process has ground to a halt with a 14th Earl'. Home responded by saying: 'I suppose Mr Wilson, when you come to think of it, is the 14th Mr Wilson.'

The Complete Roll Call
All the prime ministers from Walpole to Johnson

Robert Walpole is generally held to be the first prime minister. He also holds the record for the longest term of office at 20 years, 314 days. The term 'prime minister' was occasionally used as long ago as the seventeenth century, but it was not until the nineteenth century that it became fixed in its modern sense – that is, the person who is head of the government by dint of being the leader of the party that has a majority in parliament. Even now, the prime minister is a slightly informal term. The position is technically known as 'The First Lord of the Treasury' – and this is the title that is engraved on the brass plaque on the door of Number Ten, Downing Street.

NAME	IN OFFICE	PARTY
Robert Walpole	1721–42	Whig
Spencer Compton, Earl of Wilmington	1742–3	Whig
Henry Pelham	1743–54	Whig
Thomas Pelham-Holles, Duke of Newcastle	1754–6, 1757–62	Whig
William Cavendish, Duke of Devonshire	1756–7	Whig
John Stuart, Earl of Bute	1762–3	Tory
George Grenville	1763–5	Whig
Charles Wentworth, Marquess of Rockingham	1765–6, 1782	Whig
William Pitt (The Elder)	1766–8	Whig
Augustus Fitzroy, Duke of Grafton	1768–70	Whig
Lord North	1770–82	Tory
William Petty, Earl of Shelburne	1782–3	Whig
William Bentinck, Duke of Portland	1783, 1807–9	Whig
William Pitt (The Younger)	1783–1801, 1804–6	Tory
Henry Addington	1801–4	Tory
Lord Grenville	1806–7	Whig

Spencer Perceval	1809-12	Tory
Robert Jenkinson, Earl of Liverpool	1812-27	Tory
George Canning	1827	Tory
Frederick Robinson, Viscount Goderich	1827-8	Tory
Arthur Wellesley, Duke of Wellington	1828-30	Tory
Earl Grey	1830-34	Whig
William Lamb, Viscount Melbourne	1834, 1835-41	Whig
Robert Peel	1834-5, 1841-6	Tory
Earl Russell	1846-51, 1865-6	Liberal
The Earl of Derby	1852, 1858-9, 1866-8	Con
Earl of Aberdeen	1852-5	Tory
Viscount Palmerston	1855-8, 1859-65	Liberal
Benjamin Disraeli	1868, 1874-80	Con
William Gladstone	1868-74, 1880-85, 1886, 1892-94	Liberal
Marquess of Salisbury	1885-6, 1886-92, 1895-1902	Con
Earl of Rosebery	1894-5	Liberal
Arthur Balfour	1902-5	Con
Henry Campbell-Bannerman	1905-8	Liberal
Herbert Henry Asquith	1908-16	Liberal
David Lloyd George	1916-22	Liberal
Andrew Bonar Law	1922-3	Con
Stanley Baldwin	1923, 1924-9, 1935-7	Con
James Ramsay MacDonald	1924, 1929-35	Labour
Neville Chamberlain	1937-40	Con
Winston Churchill	1940-5, 1951-5	Con
Clement Attlee	1945-51	Labour
Anthony Eden	1955-7	Con
Harold Macmillan	1957-63	Con
Alec Douglas-Home	1963-4	Con

Harold Wilson	1964–70,1974–6	Labour
Edward Heath	1970–4	Con
James Callaghan	1976–9	Labour
Margaret Thatcher	1979–90	Con
John Major	1990–97	Con
Tony Blair	1997–2007	Labour
Gordon Brown	2007–2010	Labour
David Cameron	2010–2016	Con
Theresa May	2016–2019	Con
Boris Johnson	2019–	Con

INDEX

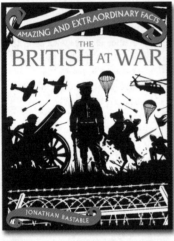

Amazing and Extraordinary
Facts Series: The British
At War
Jonathan Bastable
ISBN: 978-1 -910821-237

Amazing and Extraordinary
Facts Series: Churchill
Joseph Piercy
ISBN: 978-1 -910821-077

Amazing and Extraordinary
Facts Series: London at War
Stephen Halliday
ISBN: 978-1 -910821-084

Amazing and Extraordinary
Facts Series: Kings & Queens
Malcolm Day
ISBN: 978-1 -910821-213

For more great books visit our website at **www.rydonpublishing.co.uk**

PICTURE CREDITS